*Those oldies stations that proclaim their music "the soundtrack of your life"
are just shoveling the*  *he music of his youth,
the music of the tun* *od, but in his soul.
It formed h* *r teachers.*

*High school misadventures. Dating disasters. Troubles at home.
Procuring that illicit case of Old Milwaukee.* **8-Track Flashbacks** *is an easy, enjoyable
read. Alt's writing style is smooth, at times funny, at times serious and reflective.
He gets to the heart of things.*

BlueInk Reviews

I absolutely loved **8-Track Flashbacks**. *Once I picked it up, I couldn't put it down until
I finished reading it cover to cover, and then went back to reread some of my favorite
parts. This depiction of life in a small Midwestern town in the 1960s is so vivid, specific,
and true that I felt I was reliving my own misspent youth. I thoroughly enjoyed how the
important events in a young boy's journey to be a man—sports, girls, drinking, school,
being accepted by one's peers, and eventually striking out on one's own, were skillfully
related with humor, emotion and a wonderfully eclectic score of music of the period.*
8-Track Flashbacks *is an incredibly delightful way to reminisce about growing up as
part of the American Dream.*

Richard Riehle
Actor

Television credits include:
*ER; L.A. Law; Ally McBeal; The West Wing; Boston Legal; Quantum Leap; Roseanne;
Murder, She Wrote; Buffy the Vampire Slayer; Chicago Hope; Diagnosis: Murder;
Sabrina the Teenage Witch; Grounded for Life; Married to the Kellys; Big Stan;* and
The Young and the Restless. Riehle has also guest-starred on three of the five *Star Trek*
television series.

Riehle is probably most commonly recognized from his role as
"Tom Smykowski" in the Mike Judge film *Office Space*.

Richard Riehle was born in Menomonee Falls, Wisconsin and
attended the University of Notre Dame.

8-Track Flashbacks

Windy City Publishers
2118 Plum Grove Rd., #349
Rolling Meadows, IL 60008
www.windycitypublishers.com

Published in the United States of America
10 9 8 7 6 5 4 3 2 1

First Edition: July 2011

Library of Congress Control Number: 2011924758

ISBN: 978-1-935766-12-4

Cover Illustration and Design by Donell Hagen
Cover Production by DoubleD Graphics

Windy City Publishers
Chicago

8-Track Flashbacks

by Tom Alt

Mag Mile Books

Windy City Publishers Chicago

ATTRiBUTiON

Music was clearly the trigger for this book. The songs from our youth are a kind of time machine taking us back to high school, to playing fields and parking spots, to special moments in our lives. My own memories were evoked by and entwined with the songs of the 1960s. In telling my tales, I occasionally used a snippet from the lyrics of the song that drove the story. I did this when I realized that I could find no better words to describe what happened or how I felt than the words of a song. After all, Lennon and McCartney, among others, were among some of the greatest writers ever.

I, therefore, would like to acknowledge and express my appreciation for all those involved in bringing us the following songs from which I borrowed a line or two: the writers, performers, producers, publishers and distributors, as well as all past, present, and future owners of the rights to these great songs.

"It's Now Or Never"..................................... by Elvis Presley
"I'm Leaving It Up To You"..................... by Dale and Grace
"Leader Of The Pack" .... by The Shangri-Las
"Help" .... by The Beatles
"I'll Be There".. by The Four Tops
"Light My Fire".. by The Doors
"Groovin'"... by The Rascals
"Night Moves" .... by Bob Seger
"Honky Tonk Woman"....................... by The Rolling Stones
"Just A Little".................................... by The Beau Brummels

CONTENTS

INTRODUCTION

The Sixties
A Defining Decade

Nothing stirs the memory like music. Listen to an oldie and you are transported back to seventh grade or seventh period study hall. You're listening to the Beatles while riding shotgun in a '65 GTO, or you're once again on your first date, perhaps dancing slow and close to a song by the Righteous Brothers. This is precisely what my experience has been; I stumbled down memory lane while listening to sixties music on my iPod and found myself transported back in time to the watershed moments of a seminal decade. I was back in the 1960s, reliving some of my own stories. I was once again coming of age. I call the stories that have emerged 'faction.' They are basically true; things that happened to me while growing up in that most factious of times. But I have pared them down or embellished them at my whim, and not every detail is accurate. Some events I've moved a little in time. I wanted to equate each event to a song, and so I picked the song that was number one in America at the time of the story. Some songs seemed to dovetail nicely with the story; others were square pegs that I attempted to jam into round holes. Although this exempted some of the decade's great songs from my narrative, I liked the idea of matching the biggest song with the biggest headlines of the day. Another thing: we can all argue about what was the best song, but not about what song was number one.

Although the small events of my somewhat insular life seem inconsequential in comparison to the historic events of the sixties, the impact of that era on a young life is far-reaching and deeply profound. We were stung by the assassinations of the Kennedys and Martin Luther King, Jr. We were re-shaped by the Civil Rights Movement, the hippie movement, the Vietnam War and the anti-war protests and the ensuing violence on the campuses and in the streets of America. Artists like The Beatles, The Stones, The Doors, Bob Dylan, and Jimi Hendrix gave parents more to worry about than Elvis' sneering lips and swiveling hips. And we kids grabbed on to them. Revolutionaries pushed out rebels as heroes to many young Americans. Kids left home for co-ops, as well as college.

The music was our voice; we wanted it heard. It emboldened us, first to hold her hand, then to open our eyes and look around, while warning our parents that "something is happening here." Change was coming.

My stories occurred during the 1960s, but I hope they are more universal than just a single story about a single teenager growing up in a single decade. They may seem, on the surface, to be mostly about 'balls, boobs, and beer'—certainly three very important things in a boy's life then and, I suspect, now. But these stories are also about an adolescent's search for his place in life, about wanting badly to fit in while dreaming of getting out—about success and failure, about teen angst and embarrassment and how to deal with it all. They are ultimately about success, because no matter how mortifying an event in a teen's life seems at the time, most of us manage to grow up and get over it.

I've found I can look back and laugh at myself and I had fun writing these stories. I hope that anyone who reads them will also have fun, maybe smile, chuckle or even laugh out loud at a description of an action or event that is reminiscent of their own acts of teenage stupidity. We all stumbled on our journey through adolescence. I stumbled often, and I submit the following stories as evidence. Most, if not all, of the embarrassment was mine. The humor is meant to be self-deprecating. If any of my co-characters, co-conspirators, or co-defendants recognize themselves and are angry or embarrassed, I apologize. It was not my intent, and I think the statute of limitations on all our youthful indiscretions has long since expired.

In the spirit of full disclosure, I must admit that I very likely suffer from 'selective memory syndrome.' Author Anaïs Nin once said, "We don't see things as they are, we see things as we are." Well, this is how I see it.

I grew up during the decade of the sixties, though my wife may disagree with the whole "grew up" premise. She may be right, and the fact that I'm writing this may prove a certain reluctance to evolve. But at least I survived. the sixties were a helluva time to be a kid, and the music ... well the music was quite simply the best!

1960

News that Shook the World:

1st 50-Star Flag Raised in Philadelphia

Four Black Students Sit-In at
Woolworth's Lunch Counter
in Greensboro, N.C.

U2 Spy Plane Shot Down!
Russians Capture Pilot Gary Powers

Ike Signs Civil Rights Act

Castro Nationalizes All American—
Owned Businesses in Cuba,
Then Lands in New York to Address
The United Nations

Bill Mazeroski Is First to Win
World Series With Home Run as
Pirates Beat Yankees

But More Importantly:

Tom plays his 1st Football Game,
Faces Second and Sixteen

No. 1 Song on September 17, 1960:

"It's Now or Never"
by Elvis Presley

chapter one

IT'S NOW OR NEVER

"Down. Set. Hut, hut."

"It's now or ..." I said to myself, in my very best, pre-pubescent Elvis voice. I may even have curled my lip a little.

Terry took the snap from center, pivoted right, and pitched the ball to me. They say that great athletes have an ability to slow down the game in their minds and see things unfold as they happen. But the only thing that slowed down on that play was me, and with startling clarity I knew on that very first carry of my football life, that I was not one of them. What I saw was confusion and chaos lurking behind the three defenders already four yards into our backfield. I had started moving right with the speed of an old mule hitched to a plow in a muddy spring field. I quickly looked left, thinking of reversing my field. My helmet, however, continued to look right, and all I saw was the padding around my left ear hole. I thought perhaps one of the defenders had my facemask, but it was just that my helmet was big enough to allow my head to pivot inside of it. After the five defenders from St. Anthony climbed off, I got to my feet to see Scott and Dick laughing while the linesman signaled second and sixteen.

"... Never." I finished the thought while returning quickly to the huddle to hide. It was Sunday, September 17, 1960; a warm day under a brilliant blue sky. Castro landed in New York; I landed on my back. Mazeroski put one in the seats at Yankee Stadium; I was put on my seat.

Scott and Dick were the right guard and tackle. When the

coach said our first play would be 38, a sweep right, they thought it would be funny to lie down and watch me get killed. I didn't think it was funny. Scott and Dick were friends, classmates, and teammates. More importantly though, they were competitors for a place atop a pre-teen pantheon. Scott and Dick one, Tom zero.

I was nervous enough already, but now my first carry was a six-yard loss. I'm talking the very first carry of my football life. My career yard per carry average was now a negative six.

The aforementioned Terry, our starting quarterback, was the head coach's son (and yes you'd be right in thinking there was no coincidence there). Terry was one of our better players, and quite possibly the best choice for quarterback, but none of the other sixth graders on the St. Mary's JV football team ever had even a whiff of a chance at playing the position. I was the eleven-year-old, five-foot-four, 112-pound starting left halfback... for how long I wondered. I was big enough, strong enough, and fast enough. I excelled at playground games during recess and was often the last man standing in "pom-pom-pullaway." But I wasn't sure of my abilities and so my playground prowess didn't always translate well to the playing field.

St. Mary's in Menomonee Falls was not a wealthy parish, so our football equipment was replaced with a Scrooge-like frugality. There were limited amounts of well-fitting pads and pants, helmets and jerseys; those went to the varsity. The JV squad, like so many younger brothers, made do with hand-me-downs. So even though the best-fitting uniforms went to the starters, especially at skilled positions, including running backs, it wasn't just my helmet that was too big. My pants were so big the rest of the backfield could have joined me in them for pre-game warm-ups. They pleated at the waist and bottomed about an inch above my black high-tops instead of an inch below the knees. When I first tried them on, I looked over at the varsity and wondered who could have worn these the year before. I settled on Mr. Schmidt, the line coach, who had last exercised just after World War II. On a windy day they filled with air; all I needed were a red nose, big shoes, and a bottle of seltzer.

The answer to this problem was, of course, athletic tape, lots and lots of white athletic tape binding the pants to my not so muscular legs. Even with the tape, I defied the laws of aerodynamics by steadfastly refusing to be measurably faster. But just like the eighth graders, the skilled JV players were allowed to line their cheeks with eye black. I loved eye black. It identified me as a ball carrier and made me look, if not always feel, like a warrior.

My budding career got marginally better after that first carry, but I wasn't happy about my debut, and I couldn't let it go. I wasn't a bad athlete. In fact I was among the fastest players on the team and was at least marginally skilled. There were times when I stood out—even starred—on the gridiron. Unfortunately, with few exceptions, those times were during practice.

I was the antithesis of a gamer. During games, my spikes seemed much heavier and my muscles went on strike, all my fast-twitch fibers emigrating to my stomach. You've heard athletes talking about being "in the zone." Well, with me, the opposite seemed to happen. Instead of getting "in the zone," I zoned out. Nearly crippled by fear, I tiptoed tentatively around the edges of success. I wasn't afraid of getting hurt; I could take a hit and occasionally delivered a knockout of my own. I even played a whole season in high school with a broken wrist.

But I was afraid of messing up, of looking foolish, of not being good enough. I was terrified of second and sixteen. Terrified that my "now" would never come. I wanted it too badly. Being an athlete meant too much to me; it was how I measured my worth. To me, like many, being an athlete equated with being a man, and like size, say what you will, it mattered.

For the rest of the first quarter of that first game, our offense was Terry on a keeper right, Terry on a keeper left, Terry up the middle. As I said, he was the head coach's son, and our offense was built around getting him carries and padding his stats. I would probably have expected no less from my dad, had he been the coach. For the season, about ninety-five percent of the carries near the goal line were quarterback sneaks. If the rest of us wanted to score, we had to take it to the house from deep.

As I remember, I came close that season, once going seventy yards off tackle only to trip over the five-yard line with nary a defender in sight. I got a few more carries later in the game. I learned that I was better on the dives and the runs off tackle than the sweeps. At least I had more confidence in those plays, not trusting my speed to get outside and turn the corner. As I recall, we won the game and Terry scored all the points, but I managed to push my yards per carry average slightly into the plus column.

Menomonee Falls, Wisconsin, a dozen miles from Milwaukee and seventy or so miles north of Chicago, was middle-class Midwest. It was a beneficiary of President Eisenhower's interstate build-out. Before 1955, it was a sleepy little town of about two-thousand people, perhaps as many years as miles from the big city. After a highway became our umbilical cord to Milwaukee, we became the fastest-growing town in America, as thousands of city workers opted for backyards, barbecues, and family sedans.

By the time I was playing my first football game, the town had grown to eighteen thousand or so residents, but its skyline was still dominated by steeples and silos. That's not to say it was a one-horse town. In fact, there were two on a single farm right in the middle of town. It was, rather, a typical midwestern town transitioning from rural to suburban. It was white, mostly German, largely Protestant and conservative. It had a couple of diners, a couple of pizzerias, one movie theater, and several taverns. And here's another bit of where and when: Menomonee Falls wouldn't get its first McDonald's for another ten years.

In 1960, Wisconsin had two professional sport teams; the Milwaukee Braves and the Green Bay Packers. The Braves were halfway between a World Series win and a move to Atlanta, but were still the state's biggest sports heroes. They were the Braves of Spahn and Burdette, Crandall and Covington, Mathews and Aaron. Some people, myself included, think Henry Aaron was the best baseball player ever. But like many middle-of-the-country heroes, he was a quiet star, shining over our city and state but getting little of the fame that East Coast stars like Mantle and Mays received. This was the early days of sports television, and Aaron, the 1957 Triple-Crown winner, MVP, and World Series champion, made about $25,000 in 1960, less than many of today's stars make per at-bat.

The Packers were an ascending NFL power. When Vince Lombardi became the head coach in 1959, he had a roster that included several future Hall of Famers, including Forrest Gregg, Willie Davis, Jim Ringo, Bart Starr, Jim Taylor, and "Golden Boy" Paul Hornug. In 1960, they went 8–4, won the Western Conference title, but lost to the Philadelphia Eagles 17–13 in the NFL championship game. That team became one for the ages, winning five NFL championships in seven years, including the first two Super Bowls in 1967 and 1968.

Hornug was my idol. I wanted to be a triple-threat running back just like him. I was like him in that I wasn't particularly fast or strong or mean. And like him, I went both ways, playing safety on defense. What I needed to find out was whether or not I had the "intangibles" that Hornug had in abundance; chief among them that "nose for the end zone." My best guess at the time was that I did not. I always seemed to come up just a bit short. Pretty prescient for an eleven-year-old … don't ya think? As evidence, I submit my mishap at the five-yard line.

As I mentioned, television sports coverage was in its infancy in 1960. I knew of other stars in other sports, but never saw them perform. Like most Wisconsin kids of the time, I played the traditional sports — football, basketball, and baseball or maybe track. We had not yet been invaded by soccer (which I still think may be part of an insidious Third World plot to conquer America by putting us to sleep). Youth hockey hadn't crept over the Canadian border, and games like lacrosse were only played, as far as we could tell, at eastern prep schools. As I couldn't hit a curve, and my flirtation with basketball hadn't yet blossomed into love, I decided I wanted to be like the "Golden Boy." I must confess that it didn't hurt that he was cool—a pretty boy who got the girls. I probably should have realized how unlikely this aspiration was because, as I said, I was a good practice player while Hornug was the ultimate gamer. It was even rumored that he practiced very little because of injuries and/or lifestyle.

I remained the starting left halfback all year. The fact was that no one was good enough to take the position away from me. But I never felt secure in that. My own self-doubts contaminated the coaches' questions and criticisms, and I always thought they were looking to replace me, or failing that, at least take me out of the game plan. In their eyes, I saw the reflection of my own disappointment. I kept telling myself that all I had to do was try harder. But what I needed to do was relax and have fun. When I did that in practice or in a pick-up game, I wasn't half-bad.

Relaxing wasn't so easy for most eleven year olds, or even most high school athletes. Our coaches, with few exceptions, believed all it took to be good at their job was to be tough. I don't ever remember a coach telling me to relax and have fun. They were of the school that believed water was for sissies; they were graduates of the "run-it-off" school of coaching. Their conditioned response to almost any injury that did not include visible bone or blood was to question your manhood and tell you to run it off. "Run it off! Now get someone in here who wants to play," was a coaching cry heard on high school fields across the country. Some of us heard it in our dreams. Others of us have repeated those words at our children's practices. The words even made some of us quit.

I didn't quit though. I didn't give up. I kept playing through high school. I had the ability—not to get to the NFL or Division I, but the ability to be a good high school athlete. I could break a tackle, break the occasional big play—but I couldn't seem to break through that miasma of doubt. As I kept playing, I kept dreaming. I wanted to be the next great white running back in an NFL dominated by Jim Brown and Gayle Sayers, then Walter

Payton and O. J. Simpson—yeah, I know, but he was one helluva running back.

I wanted so badly to be regarded as a good athlete in grade school and high school, but was never, in my own estimation, good enough. Athletes were admired; they got the girls. But most of all they had self-confidence: a gravitational pull that made good things happen. I could only pretend. I even affected the slightly pigeon-toed walk a lot of good athletes had.

I still want it. I still wonder. What if I'd had a coach during those formative years who saw something worth nurturing in me, who worked to instill a confidence in me I couldn't seem to conjure up on my own? What if my dad had been around more, had played catch with me or taught me how to throw a curve or make a tackle? He was always too busy, working two jobs and doing a man's work around the house, work that always seemed to include a bottle of beer. He was a likable enough guy, but not much of an athlete. His interest in sports began and ended with the Packers.

What if I had tried harder? Even Rudy was carried off the field on the shoulders of his Notre Dame teammates. Fact is I had neither Hornug's talent nor Rudy's heart. And I still struggle with trying too hard, gripping that dream too tight, only now it's on the golf course.

If only that first carry had been different. If only on that breathtaking September Sunday in 1960, I'd have broken a tackle and looked up to see the linesman signal first and ten. Things might have been different.

But it wasn't first and ten; it was second and sixteen. There were more carries in grade school and through high school, but I never had my "now." If only I had. If only ...

1961

News that Shook the World:

JFK Becomes 35th President of
The United States

U.S. Bay of Pigs Invasion Ends
in Failure

Kennedy Dispatches "Military
Advisors" to South Vietnam

Yuri Gagarin Becomes First Man
in Space

1st Freedom Rider Action on
Interstate Bus Lines
Violence Erupts in Alabama on May 14

Roger Maris Hits 61 Homers
Breaks Babe Ruth's Record

But More Importantly:

Tom Goes on His First Date

No. 1 Song on March 17, 1961:

"Surrender"
by Elvis Presley

chapter two

SURRENDER

I splashed on some of my brother's Old Spice. Since I wouldn't be shaving for another four years, the only things that stung were my eyes. Maybe I used a little too much. My hands tingled with what may have been some kind of chemical reaction between the Old Spice and the Butch Wax left over from an attempt to tame a cowlick on the left side of my "Hollywood," a hairstyle combining a flattop with longer slick-backed sides (fenders) ending in a ducktail. The probable catalyst for all that stinging and tingling was the nervous perspiration I seemed to be producing in abundance. Wait: was that lightning I just saw in the bathroom mirror? One more dab of Butch Wax ought to do it and then I better get out of here before it starts to rain.

The reason for all the preening and perspiration was that today, March 17, 1961, my twelfth birthday, I was going to the movies with Barb. It was a Friday night and it was my first date. Barb, who sat in front of me in Mrs. Lamanscyk's sixth grade class at St. Mary's, was blonde, budding, smelled great and, if what Jane told Mary who told Steve was true, she liked me. She was also an older woman—twenty-six days older. We were going to see "Blue Hawaii" at the Menomonee Falls Theater. I was hoping that Elvis' cool would distract Barb from realizing just how freak'n scared I was. Walking to the theater, I alternately sniffed my pits and wiped my sweaty hands in the pockets of my jacket, telling myself that I'd have to remember to stop doing that once I turned the corner to the theater, especially the sniffing part.

The movie started at 7 p.m. I left my house for the four-block walk at 6:30, knowing there'd be a line for tickets. I walked down Grand Avenue, with the Menomonee River on my left, passed the carpet store at the corner and turned right on Main Street, passed Dan's Tog Shop, a local men's store where I bought my own clothes with my paper route money and where I would later work part-time while in high school. At the corner of Main and Appleton Avenue, near Lohmiller's Rexall Drugstore, I turned left, gave my pits one last sniff and made sure the collar of my jacket was up, and assumed what I imagined was a cool walk for the remaining two hundred or so yards to the theater.

Arriving at the theater, I noticed Barb wasn't there yet. I waited in the late winter chill, doing the stiff-legged dance of the miserably cold, but refusing to zip up my jacket. I may have been cold, but I was still cool. Barb came around the corner whispering and giggling with some friends. This made me even more nervous as I was certain they were laughing about me. My nose began an involuntary migration toward my left armpit. I pulled away just in time. Simultaneously, my right hand made a quick check of my fly. I just didn't have the strength to stop it. I don't think Barb or her friends noticed, but I had friends in line too, and they sure did. They were already snickering at my discomfort.

I waited for Barb to separate from the herd and then joined her in line.

"Hi," She said.

"Hi," I answered.

The conversation over, I bought two tickets at twenty-five cents a pop (I've always been a man willing to spend lavishly on a woman I care about). We went into the small theater and found seats on the aisle. It didn't have a balcony, and frankly, I was not ready for the balcony. Her friends sat three rows behind us, while a couple of my buddies sat one row behind and across the aisle. We were under surveillance.

I went to the lobby to buy popcorn and cokes, another fifty cents. I came back and handed Barb her Coke and popcorn. Our fingers touched briefly during the exchange, but I kept my cool. After all, this was not our first physical contact. Just a few minutes earlier, while standing in line, Steve yelled "Spaz," and pushed me into Barb. I brushed against her before recovering. She may have been padding.

My timing was perfect; the previews were starting. I didn't have to try to talk. There are, of course, myriad emotions at play for both a boy and a girl on a date, especially a first date. I can only speak for the boy in these situations. There is excitement and hope, but mostly there is fear, and it doesn't end. It begins days, even weeks, before the actual date.

Most of you guys know what fear I'm talking about—the fear of rejection. With the possible exception of this rejection taking place in front of his peers, the only thing a twelve-year-old boy would fear more is to be caught by those same peers (or his parents) in the bathroom ... um, not going to the bathroom. Luckily that possibility was, for me at least, extremely rare, occurring no more than two or three times a day ... sometimes four. My memory on this subject is not as firm as it once was.

The most frightening moments of this weeks-long ordeal occur between asking the girl out and waiting for the answer. During those interminable seconds, the fight or flight battle rages violently. I approached it much as a politician approaches a proposal, or a lawyer approaches a witness. That is, don't commit to a course of action or ask a question until you know the outcome or the answer. I had already initiated some back-channel contact between my people and hers. Only when assured that the answer would be yes did I ask the question. Would President Kennedy have been seen on television negotiating with Khrushchev without knowing the outcome? I think not.

With all that, I was still terrified and could have used an interpreter. I blurted out some sort of monosyllabic gibberish. The only way she could tell it was a question—I raised my voice at the end. She did say yes. I ran to relieve myself. Why do girls seem so much more at ease in these situations?

Once the request for a date is accepted, the fear of rejection morphs into an insidious, pervasive fear of nuance. During the days leading up to the date, the boy attempts to decode every word, expression and gesture for signs of excitement, nervousness or regret. Often, this task becomes overwhelming (I mean, come on, what does a twelve-year-old boy know about subtlety and nuance?) and calls for the old standby — invisibility. The boy either makes himself invisible or pretends his future date is. If he is lucky, he can pretend not to see her right up until the coming attractions.

During the date itself, this fear is at its most lethal and loathsome. A voice is now asking the boy to consider whether or not this is a "pity" date, or worse a "dare" date. This fear, of course, prevents the realization that the girl may be just as nervous and fearful. The voice seems capable of drowning all rational thought, and the body instinctively fights fire with fire by trying to drown the voice in a puddle of pubescent perspiration.

Now, should I hold her hand, put my arm around her, try to kiss her? What if she stops me? What if she doesn't!? What if I don't do it right? Up on the screen, Elvis, perpetually cool, was at a luau, serenading the girls. He was doing a lot of the heavy lifting for those of us on dates. Would Barb be willing, in the words of Elvis' current number-one record, to "surrender" to me, or would I surrender to my fears and get the hell out of there? I raced through my options. Option one: hold hands — too sweaty. Option two: put my arm around her — definite maybe. Option three: kiss her — a non-starter without either one or two, and besides, we were under surveillance. Option four: do nothing; act cool, disinterested — I was leaning heavily toward option four. It's always been one of my "go to" moves.

I looked to the screen for guidance, then … I went with two. I heard snickering behind and to my left. I'm sure Barb did too, but she didn't recoil in embarrassment or disgust. Maybe she really did like me. I briefly considered an attempt to let my hand drape low enough to brush against her right boob. No, I couldn't do that; this was the woman I loved and I wouldn't treat her like some sort of tramp. Anyway, I couldn't make it happen without lifting my left butt cheek off my seat while leaning heavily to the right, a risk I was unwilling to take.

Now I had another problem, two actually. First, by draping my right arm over the back of Barb's chair, I exposed the corresponding armpit to the air, causing an immediate and intense spike in the relative humidity. Warm front clashed with cold. There seemed to be a small storm cloud forming just above and behind us. Do I move my arm and risk insulting Barb, or risk a thunderstorm? Second, the climate change taking place on the aisle in row seventeen seemed to be causing some serious static electricity in Barb's blonde tresses. You remember the classroom experiment where you rubbed a glass rod with cat fur? Some hairs on the back of Barb's head were standing at attention. I had to drop the arm or things could really turn ugly.

When I pulled my arm away, Barb glanced at me with a look I couldn't read. Stopped again by subtlety. My hand was on my right thigh, and after a while, Barb put her hand in mine, which meant of course her hand was also on my right thigh—okay, my right knee. Though I'd love to describe how I slowly, subtly moved her hand north, I can't. Because I didn't. I had neither the courage nor the inclination to try. I'm sure she would have been disgusted, humiliated, and mortified. I would have been too. I still felt guilty about touching it myself. Anyway, like I said, I loved this women and I can't do subtlety. I was stuck halfway between innocence and insanity.

The little cloud dissipated, the barometric pressure stabilized, and the movie continued. There is some degree of safety in going to the movies on a first date. Most importantly, it minimizes the need for conversation. If I had actually had to talk to Barb at any length, I'm sure I would have run for the hills. It wasn't that I didn't really like Barb; it wasn't that at all. It was an inability to be articulate in thought or word. My mind tended to flit about like a bumblebee, landing briefly on a monosyllabic thought and then darting to the next.

Let me try to recreate for you what was probably flitting through my mind, bumble-bee-like, on the night in question. "Barb ... boob ... blonde ... boob ... boy oh boy ... boob ... boner ... boobs!" As you can see, I had a natural talent for alliteration.

The plot-challenged movie, with Elvis astride the wedding barge serenading his bride, was nearing the end, as was my first date. Elvis sang "Hawaiian Wedding Song" and Barb seemed to lean into me just a bit. She made me feel like I stood shoulder to shoulder with the King in her universe. Of course that feeling was quickly pushed aside by fear. This time the fear was that she might notice my visceral reaction to her touch (as outlined above).

That fear would soon be overwhelmed by a different dread as I began to wonder how this first date would end. What should I do next? Should I try to kiss her goodnight? The answer was no, and the fact that she would be reuniting with her friends provided perfect cover for my lack of nerve.

Should I ask to walk her home? Do I just go with the old standby—act cool and disinterested? The movie was over and we ambled up the aisle and through the lobby. I tried to stay close to Barb while her friends tried to hurry her along and Steve tried to push me into her. I had decided to end the night with a large dose of my ample coolness, but as we exited the theater and were hit by the cold night air, I froze. And by this I mean I literally froze. The nervous sweat I'd been producing the way a well-fed cow produces milk had left my clothes more than just a little damp. After less than sixty seconds in the below-freezing March air, I was covered in a thin layer of hoarfrost. I looked like a pineapple popsicle with freezer burn. I needed to get out of there, away from the strange looks I was getting from Barb's friends and the laughter of mine.

I muttered a good-bye to Barb. "See you in school."

"Bye," she said. "Thanks for the movie."

As she turned the corner, she glanced back briefly, giving me a sweet smile, and then her friends closed in, wanting to know, I'm sure, what our date had been like. Barb was the first of her friends to go on a date and the wisdom she'd just garnered from tonight's experience had to be shared. My friends covered their own envy with merciless taunts, taking particular pleasure in the fact that my clothing now crunched as I walked. What a pussy I was for sweating through the entire date. They seemed to forget that all they did was watch. I was the one who put himself on the line.

We started home, turning the corner to Main Street, past the front door of Lohmiller's, just as a couple of dads burst through the doors of Fat Jack's Tavern across the street and headed three doors down to George Webbs, a greasy spoon that served burgers and chili at night, bacon and eggs in the morning, and ulcerating coffee 24/7.

This was before Wisconsin bars like Fat Jack's had a menu or even a kitchen; they were places you went for a drink. And in our town at that time, the drink menu was pretty simple as well, Manhattans and Boilermakers (a shot and a beer—almost always a Milwaukee beer like Schlitz, Blatz or Pabst) were staples. The exceptions were, of course, the bars that served the venerable and famous "Friday night fish fry," deep-fried perch with either fries or potato pancakes and a side of slaw—good eatin.'

At Main and Grand, Steve and I separated.

"See ya, dickhead."

"Come over tomorrow."

"Can't. Gotta do chores."

"Okay. You gonna call Barb when you get home?"

"Get bent, loser."

You may have noticed that I talked more in two blocks with Steve than I had in two hours with Barb. Partly it was because I was unsure of how to talk to a girl on a date, but mostly it was that Steve and I were friends. We could talk openly and honestly about our feelings.

With a last punch on the shoulder, accompanied by a look that said "way to go," Steve continued down Main Street, crossed the river and turned left down Water Street to his home.

Steve had been my best friend since first grade. He was a pretty quiet kid, and rarely if ever mean. We played football together at St. Mary's and we skated almost every day on the frozen Menomonee River during the winter. Steve's backyard sloped down from his back door to the river, and friends were allowed to use his basement as a changing and warming house. We'd race down the snow-packed yard, jump the bank and throw ice as we slid to a stop.

Another reason I liked Steve was that he didn't compete with me for attention. He wasn't exactly Robin to my Batman, but he seemed to instinctively understand that sometimes I needed to feel like the hero. He always seemed okay with that. I understood that his pushing me into Barb earlier that evening was just something he had to do, and I'd already forgiven him. He couldn't help himself. Most boys that age just can't seem to when they get around girls, especially girls they like. It's all part of some sort of strange dance the male of the species performs to attract the female. We were just learning to dance.

I turned onto Grand and walked home. I was glad it was over, but even happier I'd done it. It was a big first step on my quest to see a real-life naked boob, or preferably two, and it was worth all the fear I had to swallow. I survived and didn't run, and for now I would refuse to succumb to the fear of Monday morning. That would overwhelm me soon enough. Right now, I just wanted to get home; I was freezing my butt off.

I recently looked at a picture of my daughter and her friends before their eighth grade "May Ball." The girls all looked so pretty and grown up; frighteningly so from a father's perspective. The boys, however, looked like thirteen- and fourteen-year-old dorks, way too young and immature to be in the company of those young ladies. I wondered if it had been the same way back when Elvis was still King.

In 1961, especially in small towns like Menomonee Falls, we were still holding on pretty hard to the 1950s. We had not yet invaded Vietnam. The British had not yet re-invaded America with their music. We still clung to the innocence of soda fountains, drive-in restaurants, and Hula-Hoops. We didn't text or twitter and didn't wage anonymous wars against another's character over the Internet.

And yet I think the answer is yes. We, like the twelve- to fourteen-year-old boys of today, were dorks, too insipid and immature to be in the company of young ladies. They grow up much faster than boys. They always have. I think that's what attracts us in the first place.

Today, I can reluctantly admit that I, too, may possibly have been a dork. I was a self-absorbed twelve-year-old boy, unaware of the world around him. And I was probably way too young and immature to be on a date with Barb. But I was in the first steps of my journey toward manhood. That journey has been for the most part a success, albeit with many stumbles along the way. Also, the fear has never completely gone away. Every first date, every intimate moment required me to first swallow at least a little fear. Even now, nearly a half-century after that first date and with a woman I've known and loved for over thirty years, there is still a little fear — fear of rejection

But that fear has always been overcome by a stronger urge — the quest to see a real boob or two. By the way, my first boob came a couple of years after that first date (although who it belonged to shall remain my little secret).

1962

News that Shook the World:

NASA: John Glenn Becomes First
American to Orbit Earth

Wilt Chamberlain Scores 100 Points
In an NBA Game in Philadelphia's Victory
Over the New York Knicks

Students for a Democratic Society
(SDS) Complete Port Huron Statement

Changes in Africa: Algeria, Rwanda,
Burundi & Uganda Gain Independence

Marilyn Monroe Dead in Probable
Suicide

James Meredith is First African-
American to Register at
The University of Mississippi

U.S. Imposes Arms Blockade on Cuba:
Kennedy Ready for Soviet Showdown

But More Importantly:

Tom Scores 2 in Basketball While Wearing
Clown Shoes

No. 1 Song on January 6, 1962:

"The Lion Sleeps Tonight"
by The Tokens

chapter three

THE LION SLEEPS TONIGHT

My older brother chortled wickedly; tee-heed sadistically. "I heard that was one hell of a shot. A little scared, Cowardly Lion?"

Oh great: the last thing I needed was to be given a new nickname by my loving, always supportive, prick of an older brother. This would be hard to live down. He sure as hell wasn't going to keep this between us — wouldn't be nearly as much fun.

The reason for my new moniker: yesterday, Saturday January 6, 1962, I stepped to the free-throw line to shoot the first end of a one-and-one.

But let me set the scene for you: it was my first game of organized team basketball, playing for the St. Mary's seventh grade team. It was our fifth game overall and the first in our conference. I'd missed the first four games with a sprained left ankle, spending much of my Christmas break on crutches. So this was the very first official shot attempt of my basketball life.

Before my injury, I had been named a starting forward. Back then a basketball team consisted of a center, two forwards and two guards. There was no 1, 2, 3, 4, or 5. There was no small and power forward. There were just guards, forwards and a center. I suppose I was, in today's terms, a power forward, as I was more a rebounder and defender than a scorer.

Having grown to five feet eight inches and weighing in at 130 pounds, I was not exactly the personification of power, but I was a power forward, albeit one who was reluctant to shoot.

Basketball was now my second sport. I had two seasons of grade school football under my belt and was ready to be a multi-sport star, my flaming mediocrity as a football running back notwithstanding.

Back at the free-throw line, the referee handed me the ball for the front-end of a one-and-one. I felt a tremor; my hands shook slightly and there was a rumbling in what I would later learn was my colon. It seemed things might be breaking loose. I was afraid to bend my knees as I knew I should. Choosing to focus instead on tightening my sphincter, I was afraid to follow through on the shot.

The result, as you can imagine, was an air ball that never reached the rim. Though neither the first nor the last air ball thrown up by a seventh grader, this one became noteworthy because of what immediately ensued. As I said, the ball fell woefully short. It missed the rim, and bounced out the front door, which was opened while the ball was in the air, bounced down the front steps, rolled across the street and came to rest in a snow bank.

We were playing ball in what had been St. Agnes Church in Butler, Wisconsin; a little blue-collar enclave attached to the northwest corner of Milwaukee and a few miles southeast of Menomonee Falls. St. Agnes had recently built a new church and because the school had no gym, they converted the tiny old church into a basketball court. The court ran lengthwise along the tiny church, one basket where the altar once stood and one facing the front door. I was shooting free throws toward that door.

Thus, a simple air ball became something much more, something others would no doubt remember just as I would desperately try to forget. I think I recall the poor misguided ball splitting "God Rays" as it dove through the open door. There may even have been a little weeping and gnashing of teeth. Though I didn't personally weep, I'm fairly certain I gnashed. The fact that the ball was returned from the snow bank by a late-arriving father with a big grin on his face and wiped off by an openly laughing referee just made things worse.

Up to this point in the game, I had played okay. I defended, rebounded and gave up the ball to my more offensive teammates (decide for yourself whether that was a pun). However, the air ball was not my first faux pas. As I entered the gym before the game, I reached into a tattered old navy gym bag and realized, to my horror and embarrassment, that I didn't have my basketball shoes. Of course, I couldn't call someone to bring them to me because there was no phone in the gym, and this being 1962, I had left my cell phone in the future. I tried to finesse the problem and entered the pre-game layup line in my gym socks, hoping no one would notice. Obviously, that wasn't going to work.

"Alt." Coach Ullsperger called me over. "Where are your shoes?"

"In my dad's car, Coach."

"Is he coming?"

"I think so."

"You know I can't let you play without shoes." After a moment's hesitation, he added: "Here, take mine."

"Thank you sir." I think Coach was trying hard not to laugh. Having decided to let the opportunity for a lesson pass, he handed me his white Converse All Stars. This was, I came to realize, a terrific gesture. I would be starting my first basketball game after all, and not sitting at the end of the bench wiggling my shoeless toes. On the other hand, I wore a size nine; coach's Chuck Taylor's were a size twelve or thirteen. They looked like clown shoes, and of course, my feet bounced around in them when I moved. I practically came out of them every time I jumped.

I had a frightening flashback to the fall of 1960, and sensed a common theme. Just like my oversized sixth grade football pants, my basketball shoes practically screamed for a seltzer bottle and a red nose.

That wasn't the worst of it though. You know how a person can simply feel where he is, for example, he knows that his feet are on the right side of the baseline without having to look down and check. Well, early in the second quarter, we were awarded the ball after our opponent turned it over. My job was to in-bound the ball to one of our guards. And yes, my feet were out of bounds, as they needed to be when I threw in the ball.

The problem was that my shoes were two or three inches over the line. The whistle blew and the ball was awarded back to St. Agnes. Off the inbound pass, a St. Agnes player drove to the basket. I rotated defensively, showing a highly developed understanding of the game's defensive principles as well as a great instinct for the game, and stepped between him and the rim. Another whistle and I was called for a foul. You see, my opponent tripped over my shoe—not my foot mind you, but my shoe. I never touched the guy. So much for sound defensive principles.

The next whistle beckoned me to the bench, where I spent the rest of the first half. Just before the second half started my dad came in. When I got his attention, I wiggled my shoeless feet in his direction. He rolled his eyes while moving his ubiquitous toothpick from one side of his mouth to the other. I told him my shoes were in the car. With one more roll of the eyes and another lap of his toothpick, he flipped me the keys.

I ran into the near-zero air, found the car and grabbed my sneakers. The light layer of sweat I'd worked up in the gym was now a glaze. I was freezing. Back in the gym, I changed into my sneakers and joined my teammates for lay-ups.

The second half resumed and I suffered no further embarrassment. I scored on a put-back off an offensive rebound, the only shot I attempted all game, and we won handily. After Coach's post-game talk, I left with my dad. I don't recall him coming to any other games in any sport, whether I was playing for St. Mary's or later in high school. He wasn't around much, but he came to this one, and he brought my sneakers.

"Let's stop for a beer." Apparently my dad knew the bars in Butler. So on this cold, clear winter day, we walked into the musty darkness of a tavern that smelled of cigarettes and spilled beer, and sat side by side at the bar. My dad sipped a Miller High Life without taking either his toothpick or his Viceroy out of the corners of his mouth. How did he do that? I had a cherry Coke and munched on salted peanuts and threw the shells on the floor along with everybody else. How cool is that? I watched my dad, who seemed to sit a barstool well. He wasn't a tall man, only five feet nine inches, and was thick from the waist down, with a working man's forearms. He had a certain lazy charm and liked to tell a joke. He was a "pull my finger" kind of guy, the right kind of guy with whom to share a beer. Or a cherry Coke.

It was neat to spend time alone with my dad. We didn't talk about the game or how I played. In truth, my dad didn't know a whole lot about sports and I don't think he was much of a basketball fan. In fact, we talked very little. That was okay. The silence didn't need to be filled with meaningless chatter and it was nice just being there together.

I was glad we won, but still pretty embarrassed about my free throw. Some of the guys on the team gave it to me good, especially (and not surprisingly) the ones who thought they should be playing ahead of me.

I didn't sleep very well that night. My mind was too busy previewing all the shit that was coming my way. Even though I had a pretty good imagination, I had underestimated the psychic carnage to come. The next morning, while sunlight stabbed at my eyelids, my older brother poked at my psyche. How had he found out so fast?

With hands at his throat in the international signal for choking, he teased; "nice shot—a little scared?" For the next several weeks, I was the "cowardly lion." I was only grateful that he was in high school and not coming to St. Mary's tomorrow. In the back of my mind though, I feared he'd find a way to let my classmates know my new nickname. He didn't. Thank you for that.

The rest of the season went well. We were undefeated in conference and were 12–4 overall. I was new to basketball but came to love the game. By the following year, we fielded an eighth grade squad that dominated most opponents with a line up of five players all the same height—five feet nine inches. We won our first game 49-2, our second 56-6, and rolled through most of our schedule.

Going into our last game, the Waukesha County Catholic Championship against our nemesis, the rich kids from St. Mary's of Elm Grove, we were 19-0. We lost that game in overtime, but I remember it as one of the best games I ever played and one of the most fun I ever played in. I continued to play the game in high school and then recreationally until just a few months ago when I turned sixty. With few exceptions, I have remained a reluctant shooter.

A few times in high school, I was pulled from a game for not shooting. In one such game, I came off the bench as a sixth man and was "feeling it." I made five shots in a row from the left wing. Then when pressured, I put it on the floor and scored at the rim. Six for six, I put up a seventh shot. It went in and out. Just like that, the balloon seemed to burst and I didn't attempt another shot. That was the most points I ever scored in an official game. Even with that kind of success, I never became a confident shooter. I'm not sure why. Confidence is a very slippery sort of thing. Even in my fifties, I didn't develop the "old man's game" of just setting and shooting. I rebounded, defended, banged, and passed.

I wasn't scarred by that first air ball, but maybe I was scraped up a little. Unlike scars, scrapes scab, heal, and disappear. Perhaps that first air ball is in part why I never became a confident shooter. But other than the humor of the situation viewed in hindsight, what I most remember about that first game is that I got back in the game. My dad showed up and brought my sneakers. As I mentioned, it was the only game he ever came to. Serendipitous? Perhaps.

My coach put me back in the game despite my first half problems. Should I be grateful? Absolutely. I got back in the game and stayed in the game for about forty-seven years. It's given me a lot of pleasure and a little pain, and more than a few embarrassing moments. Now, I can laugh at myself. Then? Well then the embarrassment was almost unbearable, almost overwhelming. The operative word here is "almost," because, like most embarrassing adolescent moments, that feeling didn't last very long.

It was soon forgotten, replaced by some other stupid or embarrassing incident involving me or some other poor, zit-faced, brain-addled, hormonally-charged adolescent. But like Saturday night after the game, that Sunday night, things were still pretty raw, still very about me. The lion didn't sleep that night either.

1963

News that Shook the World:

Alabama Governor George Wallace Vows:
"Segregation Now. Segregation Forever."

JFK Delivers Landmark Civil
Rights Address

Martin Luther King Jr. Proclaims:
"I Have a Dream"

Betty Friedan's "The Feminine Mystique"
Catalyzes Women's Movement

U.S. Involvement in
South Vietnam Escalates

Assassin Kills Kennedy
Lyndon Johnson Sworn In

Beatles Release First Two
Singles in U.S.
Elvis Supplanted as King
By Dylan and Beatles

But More Importantly:

Tom Throws a Punch & Gets Suspended
Is Alone and Adrift

No. 1 Song on November 25, 1963:

"I'm Leaving It Up To You"
by Dale & Grace

chapter four

I'M LEAVING IT UP TO YOU

It's 12:40 p.m., Monday, November 25, 1963, and I'm eating lunch in the cafeteria at Menomonee Falls High School, just as I had been the Friday past. I'm a freshman, and this is my lunch period. But today, I'm in a different time and place—a different world. Today there is an almost suffocating silence; it hangs heavily, a hall monitor warning against the usual chatter, the juvenile horseplay. It is as if we are ... no, we are at a wake, and we have to act ... no, we have to be more grown up.

Last Friday, November 22, 1963, at 12:40, Mr. Sirianni, the principal grabbed us by the throat and told us, "President Kennedy has been shot!" Today, many of us still have trouble swallowing. That announcement seemed to suck all the air out of the cafeteria; it left us in a vacuum. When that vacuum was compromised by a sob from the girl at the next table, fear, disbelief, doubt, and anger poured in and the atmosphere was changed—for good.

That evening, our new president, Lyndon Baines Johnson, spoke to us solemnly of the tragedy and forcefully of the future. At fourteen, I had little perspective, but as great a man as Johnson may have been, I had a strong sense—in the same way that smoke suggests fire—that he was not my president. JFK was all sparkle and promise, a new convertible. Johnson was as stodgy as a four-door sedan, the new principal about whom we knew nothing and who conducted business behind closed doors. He didn't speak to us or for us, and he certainly wouldn't listen to us. While JFK, like rock-and-roll, seemed ours, Johnson belonged to our parents. He was the chaperone at our dance, pulling us apart. It felt as though the old guard has wrested back power from the upstart.

The tragic events in Dallas have spawned as many conspiracy theories as any event in history. If in fact, the old guard decided they were not yet ready to give the country over to the next generation of leaders and took back Camelot from a young King Arthur, they made a terrible mistake. Even if not complicit, going back to business as usual was in itself an error of enormous proportions. We would not cede so quietly as they may have expected. We'd been awakened, and we began to look at our elders differently, more skeptically.

That singular moment in time was our generation's reminder of the sometimes-senseless cruelty of our world. It belittled our naiveté, mocked our innocence. It pulled us out of the fifties, making anachronisms of our sock hops and Hula-Hoops. We washed the Brylcreem from our hair and let it down. We put away our 45s about puppy love and sang along to edgier anthems. Now all this didn't happen overnight. It took a while.

Menomonee Falls, Wisconsin was a pretty damn conservative town, but even there some of the kids went from "greaser" to "collegiate" and, by 1968, some of them even moved on to "hippie" status. Kennedy's death certainly didn't light the fire of radicalism in America, but gave it oxygen and the fire spread, even to Menomonee Falls. JFK was our Arthur and we aspired to sit at his Round Table, to pledge our fealty and our sword to his endeavors. Quite simply, he got us interested. So even though the Round Table was broken and our hero had fallen, our interest did not wane. On the contrary, his death would steel that interest in a forge fired by anger and mistrust.

African Americans marched into Southern classrooms. We marched on Washington. Later we would march against the war in cities and on campuses and we would be bloodied. We would march into Chicago in 1968 to demonstrate against the politics as usual of the Democratic National Convention; march into war when Mayor Daley gave the "shoot-to-kill" order to the Chicago police, the casualty count high, the wall between them and us made higher still. We would march into the country to commune with nature and into the "Haight" for the summer of love, and finally as the decade came to an end, five-hundred thousand of us would march through upstate New York, to a place called Woodstock. It was up to us now.

I didn't march — yet. I did, however, observe, even empathize with the marchers and with those who chose to "drop out." It was my fear of drugs that caused me to keep this new world at arm's length. I have never understood the concept that being stoned was illuminating. My own observation is that the opposite is true; drugs only muddy one's vision. I was afraid of drugs, afraid of losing control. Later on, I would experiment a bit. I tried nothing more potent than pot, which, unlike some, I did inhale, and hash, which just made me paranoid. So that was no fun.

But I have marched ahead a bit. On Monday, November 25, 1963, we all were still numb. And I was still a high school freshman in a small town in the Midwest.

It generally takes very little persuasion to get a teenager to rebel against authority. I had a life-long mistrust of authority. I suppose it was rooted in the fact that I had learned to look over my shoulder for the backhand that would inevitably come. I had learned to fear and mistrust the one person I should have been able to rely on. Teachers, parents, police, and parents of friends often seemed arbitrary and capricious in their treatment of kids, especially kids who were closing in on puberty. It's as if the very act of growing up was a challenge to their authority, a reminder that it wouldn't be theirs much longer. They treated us much as the old guard treated Kennedy, with a modicum of latitude so long as we remembered who was really in charge. If we forgot, the retribution could be swift, and sometimes fierce.

This was a time that still tolerated corporal punishment, and it wasn't just parents. Teachers and coaches were just as quick to lay a hand on anyone in their charge. And no child in my memory ever threatened to sue. Some fought back, but nearly all lost, either immediately or later on.

In addition, I have always been a bit of a smart-ass, a class clown. I've managed (and I know this is hard to believe) to occasionally get on the nerves of those given the responsibility to watch me, teach me, coach me, work with me, and yes even marry me. And I saw JFK's assassination as just another example of how the grown ups were messing up the world. Just another reason not to trust them.

Not only did I lose my leader, I lost my hero. He packed up and walked out the very next day. The day after JFK was shot and killed, my dad left for good. I was beginning to lose my faith. Apparently my dad was not, in fact, the smartest, strongest, bravest man in the world. For years, I had believed that he was all those things, and I chose to believe that long after I knew it wasn't so. But, he wasn't smart enough to make our lives better, wasn't strong enough to make our mother stop beating us, and wasn't brave enough to stay. He was my hero just because he was my dad. Isn't that why kids sucked on those candy cigarettes with the red tips and wanted a cherry in their kiddie cocktail? Isn't that why young boys tried to walk and talk like their old man? Our dads were our heroes. But now, like JFK, my dad was gone. His was a less than heroic retreat. Oh well, no hard feelings, right?

In truth, I didn't really blame him for finally leaving our mother, but wondered what took so long. He had had one foot out the door for years. He was desperate to be free of the woman to whom he'd once pledged his undying love, or at least agreed to marry. She was nearly impossible to live with. She sucked the joy from our family, greedily, like a vampire sucks blood. Clearly, they didn't belong together. But, by leaving our mother, he was also leaving us. That was harder to forgive.

Our house, its oxygen burned up by anger and violence, was oppressive and left us gasping for air. He didn't ever really protect us from our mother's bile. If we were beaten while he was gone, he'd sometimes call her on it, then they'd argue violently; he'd storm out and she'd be back at us, blaming us for the argument and releasing her newly recharged rage. And now, at fourteen, I didn't really need his physical protection. I'd decided long ago I wouldn't be beaten anymore. I could hold her off, or leave like Dad did.

He didn't teach us much about sports, no tips on how to throw or catch a ball, no example of how to compete. He did occasionally take us fishing though, an upper-Midwest rite of passage. Like I said, he was my hero just because he was my dad.

He did teach me something by leaving all those times things got ugly. He taught me that a real man doesn't leave when his exit puts the smaller and weaker in the line of fire. So I didn't leave. Maybe he stuck around until he thought one of us could stand up to the demands that come with being a man, stand up to our mother, stand between her and the younger kids. I am the second of five, with a brother two years older, a sister three years younger, and two even younger brothers. Maybe he stayed until he was sure I wouldn't leave. Maybe he just couldn't take it anymore. Maybe he had somewhere else to go, someone else to go to. Most probably, it was a bit of all these. His leaving said: "I can't do this anymore." Like the lyrics of the song, he seemed to say, "That's why I'm leaving it up to you. You decide what you're gonna do."

The next Thursday was Thanksgiving. In 1963, it was a national holiday that still stood on its own, not yet the first day of Christmas. We had a ritual during those years. On Monday, we would bring home a Butterball turkey to be served on Thursday with pork sausage stuffing, mashed potatoes and gravy, sweet potatoes, green beans, and cranberry sauce. The meal ended with pumpkin pie and was a typically gluttonous American family tradition

But the dinner was more fractious than festive, more fright fest than feast. We kids peeled potatoes, opened cans and set the table, all with one eye on the clock. The silence was oppressive, as if the oven was open all day in the small kitchen made even smaller by the anger that hung heavier than the aromas.

At 5:00 p.m. on that Thanksgiving in 1963, our mom put the food on the table, made herself a Manhattan and left the kitchen without a word. We just stared—at each other, at the food. I looked toward the darkened living room and could see the glowing red tip of her Parliament reflected in the front window. Other than the occasional tinkling of ice in her drink, the old house was silent. Even the floorboards seemed afraid to squeak, the heat ducts afraid to clatter, the mice afraid to skitter.

"Eat before it gets cold," our mom warned. Tapping spoons and scraping forks punctured the silence as air seeped slowly back into the room.

"Come on," I whispered, starting to eat.

After dinner, all the kids wanted to help with dishes. I put away leftovers, my sister washed and my little brothers dried. Then I put away the dishes handed to me one at a time, the little ones not wanting to be more than a few feet away for more than a few seconds.

The dishes done, the little ones looked at me as if to say, now what? Our one black and white television, a large piece of furniture with a small screen, was in the living room. Its black face reflected another red cigarette tip alongside the one in the window, making it seem like two people were smoking in unison. The quiet was foreboding.

I went to the hall closet, dug out the Monopoly game, and set it up on the kitchen table. I figured the game could take us to, or at least near to, bedtime. Ever tried to play a board game without making any noise? It isn't easy and we weren't successful. The first warning was the quick rise then disappearance of that little red glow. It was a UFO that hovered, shimmered, then darted at an otherworldly speed. We were, I feared, under attack. Almost as quickly as the red dot disappeared, our mother was at the kitchen table. After mixing another Manhattan, she swept the game off the table and onto the floor, then faded back into the dark.

We had apparently committed the unpardonable sin of trying to have a little fun. At least we now had something to do to take us to bedtime. Hell, it would take a while just to get the tiny little iron out from under the fridge. I stayed between my mom and my younger siblings until she retreated back to the living room. It sure felt like it was up to me.

After cleaning up the game pieces and returning it to the hall closet, the younger kids quietly got ready for bed.

"Why is Mom always so mad at us?" Bob whispered in an afraid-of-the-dark voice.

"She's not mad at you," I answered.

"Who's she mad at?"

"I don't know. Maybe she's mad at herself. Think you can sleep?"

I've mentioned an older brother and you might be wondering where he was. Well, he was a bit more like my dad. He found it easier to leave. He had a girlfriend and spent almost all his time with her. Good for him — not always so good for me. I needed to find a girlfriend.

Monday didn't come nearly soon enough. It wasn't so much going to school that I looked forward to, but getting out of the house. Four-day weekends pretty much sucked. Mom was getting ready for her job as a secretary at a small local firm. Her schedule was most important and any lapses on our part met with an angry warning from the staccato of high heels goose-stepping across the kitchen's linoleum floor. While staying out of her way, I helped my younger siblings pack their brown-bag lunches and made sure they got out the door. They had a three-block walk to St. Mary's. I went back to good old Menomonee High.

Like many in America, I felt a personal loss when JFK was shot and killed. As a kid, it was more or less a feeling of abandonment. My distrust of and discomfort with authority was fed by the sense that I'd just been abandoned by two of the most important men in my life: one a very public role model, a bright star, the other a man I wished had been more of a role model for me. I began to view my teachers and coaches with even more skepticism than before. They weren't going to do shit. They didn't seem to care. Well, I'd just turn up my collar and give them my best wise-ass comment and "who needs 'em" look.

Basketball practice started that Monday. I've already mentioned that I loved sports and desperately wanted to be a good athlete. I felt the need to be perfect, and when it turned out I wasn't, I thought I wasn't any good at all. Then I became angry with the coaches. They weren't coaching me. They weren't encouraging me. They didn't like me. They were playing favorites. It was like Johnson's presidency: politics as usual. Despite this, I looked forward to practices every day after school. I was still a jock, one of the cool kids, and, more importantly, I was staying out of the house.

I wasn't starting, but I was the first player off the bench, playing a fair number of minutes. In the fall, I had broken my right wrist during football. I came back too early, having decided to keep playing with it broken. I told the coaches that it had been diagnosed as a sprain. Of course, it didn't heal properly. It needed to be re-broken and repaired surgically, which I hadn't done. I kept playing football that fall, and of course the wrist didn't heal.

While playing basketball, my wrist would get swollen and sore and my range of motion was severely restricted. I played through this and expected the coaches to applaud my guts. They didn't. This pissed me off. But you see, I didn't tell them about the wrist for fear that my season would be over. I expected to be lauded for playing through an injury they didn't even know about.

Midway through the season, during a home game against Nicolet, I was on the floor in the second quarter. I made a steal and raced up court on a breakaway. A Nicolet defender retreated, and instead of contesting my lay-up, he went down and took out my legs at the knees. It was clearly a dirty play. I went hard and headlong into the wall and while trying to break my fall, re-broke my right wrist. I was hurting and furious and looked to the bench, expecting my coach to go to bat for me. I expected to see him on his feet, screaming for a flagrant foul call and an ejection of the Nicolet player. He just sat there; said and did nothing.

When I looked at the Nicolet player, he just grinned at me wickedly, triumphantly. I snapped. I dropped him with a left. I was, of course, ejected from the game, as my opponent should have been. But I didn't care. Some response was required, and—once again—I felt like it was up to me.

Being ejected from the game wasn't so bad. Actually it was kind of cool, almost heroic in a warped sort of teenage way. But when I got back to the bench, my coach told me to leave the floor. I was stunned and shuffled off to the locker room. When the team came into the locker at halftime, the coach exploded.

"What the hell are you still doing here, Alt? The locker room is for the team only. Drop your uniform off on the way out. You're through."

What was it about me and grownups? Did they not get me or did I not get them? What were the rules and why didn't they tell me when they changed? Why didn't a single adult have my back? Why was it always up to me?

The following week, I went in to see the coach and asked to be allowed back on the team. The answer was no. Because of my wrist, I couldn't play anyway, but I hoped to be allowed to attend practices and sit on the bench during games. I explained that I knew what I did was wrong and apologized. I wondered why the actions of the Nicolet player were not punished. What he'd done was clearly dirty and with, in my mind, intent to injure. Again, the answer was no. He didn't want someone like me on his bench. I left the office feeling isolated and alone—but acting unfazed.

I couldn't say to the coach that I felt abandoned; that I needed to think that there was an adult I could count on. I didn't know how. I didn't know if anyone would have listened. If I had, the coach probably would have sat me down and explained that I could learn from my mistake and—wait for it—what I would learn from it would be up to me. Instead, what I felt strongly was that my mistake came directly from his mistake in not defending me. What I could do was look at him with a practiced lip-curling sneer, pull up the collar on my jacket and leave his office showing him I was just fine with it being up to me.

1964

News that Shook the World:

President Johnson Declares War
on Poverty

Berkeley Free Speech Movement Born

Nikita Khrushchev Deposed as
Leader of USSR

Beatles Lead Second British Invasion

Second Vatican Council Condemns
the "Pill"

Three Civil Rights Workers Murdered in
Mississippi by Klan, Cops.

But More Importantly:

Tom Has a Brief Encounter
with Crime

No. 1 Song on November 21, 1964:

"Leader of the Pack"
by The Shangri-Las

chapter five

LEADER OF THE PACK

slid into the backseat. Even though I'd be the first one out, Russ had called shotgun and that was that. We left the parking lot of The Grill, a hamburger joint down the hill from the high school and next door to the Falls Lanes bowling alley. We drove the three miles to Pop Gissal's, a little general store at the eastern edge of Menomonee Falls.

The date was Saturday, November 21, 1964. I had played my last football game of the season the night before and basketball practice would start on Monday. Despite being booted from the basketball team last year, I would be allowed to try out for the sophomore team. But I would be carrying some heavy baggage; the coaches had not forgotten last year. I would need to keep my nose clean. It was 5:45 p.m. on a cold and damp autumn evening, with daylight fading fast. We wanted to arrive at Pop's just before he closed at 6:00 p.m.

In the back seat with me were Al and Mike. Al was a kind of Fonz; white T-shirt, leather jacket, and black biker boots. He also had a carefully coiffed Phil Everly pompadour. He didn't talk much: was always cool, and never in a hurry. He was in fact a good kid, and smart as a whip.

Mike, like me, played football. A defensive lineman, he was a bit fleshy, a bit lazy, and he carried himself with the easy comfort of someone more than a little well off. He laughed often, his eyes disappearing in his round jolly face.

Russ rode low in the front seat. He was funny, loud, and vulgar. An unapologetic horn-dog, he chased the girls tirelessly and seemed to get away with saying things to them the rest of us could not. We were all sophomores at Menomonee Falls High School, all fifteen years old.

Behind the wheel of the '58 baby blue Chevy Bel Air convertible taking us east on Appleton Avenue was the leader of this pack, Grif. He, too, was a sophomore, but he was seventeen. That alone should have made us question our decision to follow. He'd been held back twice in grade school, or, as we said then, he'd flunked. But he had a license and a car, and it wasn't just any car: he had a convertible. Though it seemed we pushed it as often as we rode in it, when the body was shined up and the top was down, it was still a very cool car. The five of us called ourselves "The Big 5."

Several months ago, Grif had changed his look from Greaser to "collegiate" and today he sported white Levis, a madras shirt, no socks, penny loafers complete with pennies, and a hooded windbreaker. He also left a trailing scent of Canoe wherever he went, though you'd find more fuzz on a peach. Although he now wanted to look like a Beach Boy instead of Elvis, Grif was still a greaser at heart.

On the Chevy's scratchy AM radio, the Shangri Las were singing "look-out, look-out, look-out" from their number one hit, "Leader of the Pack." Perhaps I should have been listening to their warning, but I listened to Grif instead when he turned off the radio and said: "Let's do this."

The other four guys and I hadn't become friends until high school. They were public school kids, and I went to St. Mary's. In the year or so since we all started attending the only high school in town, we'd gotten pretty tight and seemed to be the guys the girls in our class most wanted to be around. We were pretty damned cool. At least we thought we were cool and, many a confused, horny fifteen-year-old wanted to grow the number of our group.

Most of the time, we did what nearly every other teen in nearly every other small town was doing; we dated, we drank when we could get a hold of some beer, and we cruised when we could get enough money together for gas and Grif's '58 actually started. When we couldn't, we hung out at The Grill, where we weren't always required to spend money.

Tonight, however, we were about to do something completely different. We were on a caper. Somehow, we had decided to "knock off" Pop Gissal's to get some liquor for this Saturday night and a few down the road. So, no I didn't keep my nose clean.

I can't tell you what was in the other guys' minds, but I didn't really think of this as immoral or illegal. I saw it as a lark, something done on a dare, something to get away with. I knew it was wrong and it could get me in a shit-load of trouble, but we weren't going to hurt anybody. The three bottles of booze we were planning to lift had a total retail value of maybe $15.00. Still, I was scared of being caught. But I was more scared of backing down.

We wanted to get to Pop's just before he closed for the night. Our thinking was he'd be in a hurry to get us in and out of the store. It was my job to go in first, alone. I was going to ask Pop for a couple of cold quarts of Coke. (Try saying that three times fast while you're scared out of your wits!) Pop would have to go into the back room to retrieve the Cokes from the cooler. The boys would come in, snatch a couple of bottles off the shelf and leave. I would pay for the Cokes and join them in the getaway car, which hopefully wouldn't stall. I pictured us pushing the Chevy down Appleton Avenue, trying desperately to outrun the police.

The determination to appoint me as the front man was made partly because Pop Gissal didn't know me, but primarily because I looked like the "nicest kid." I was Ritchie Cunningham to Al's Fonzie. What we didn't take into consideration was the fact that I was probably the least likely to succeed in a life of crime and I would've been voted the most likely to soil himself in this situation.

I don't know which of The Big 5 had the most to lose if we got caught. None of us was exactly wanted by the Menomonee

Falls Police Department, but some of the others may have been on their radar for truancies and the like.

Come to think of it, maybe I was the one with the most to lose. I was class president, an athlete, and a pretty good student who hoped to go to college and needed a scholarship to get there. So why was I doing this? What the hell was I thinking? How the hell do I know? But there was a little bit of a thrill in being that kind of scared. In a way I was losing my virginity. Or maybe it was purely and simply a matter of wanting to fit in, but I wouldn't have admitted that to myself then. (And I'll still vigorously deny it today!)

We pulled into the small gravel lot two doors down from Pop's exactly eight minutes before closing time. I got out of the car and tried desperately to stride casually into the store. But there was very little glide in my stride that night and my knees were knocking. It was a cold night, but I was sweating, and the icy air made me shiver. I stepped into the tiny shop and looked at the candy to give the gang time to enter the shop, then carried a bag of Twizzlers to the counter and asked Pop for a couple of cold quarts of Coke. He hesitated, eyeing me suspiciously over his half-glasses. It was a look that could wipe the smirk off the most confident kid's face, and I was far from confident. Then he went into the back room. I sensed a liquification of my bowels beginning, but puckered and stood strong.

Al, Russ, and Mike each grabbed a quart of booze off the shelves and turned to leave. Al, I swear to God, carried his bottle out in front of him, studying the label. I thought for a second he might come back and exchange it for something else. The others stashed the bottles beneath their jackets and they all exited the premises.

Pop came back around the corner.

"Where are your friends?"

"They weren't my friends. They left."

"Don't tell me you don't know them. They came in with you."

"No they didn't. I'm alone."

"What did they steal? Get them back in here, or I'll call the police."

"They weren't with me. I don't know if they took anything."

"Get them back here."

All the while, Pop held the two quarts of Coke in his hand, refusing to put them on the counter.

"Are you going to sell me the two cold Coke of quarts or not?"

"I'm going to call the police."

"All I wanted was a couple Cokes of cold quarts. If you won't sell them to me, I'm leaving."

"You stay right where you are, you punk. I'm calling the police," he commanded as he reached around the corner for the phone.

"Quar qua quoke," I stammered. Then I was silent. I needed to get out of there before I confessed to killing Abel.

This had already been an eternity and now I plodded through a quicksand of terror toward the front door. When I got outside, Al was standing next to the passenger door fixing his hair. Are you kidding me? Apparently, he'd called shotgun.

"He knows," I said. "He's calling the police."

Now this is absolutely true and very important to the story. Just then, we heard a siren. They were coming to get us, casting their dragnet, closing in on the notorious Big 5. Al slammed the car door shut and the two of us took off on foot. The '58, with the booze on the floor beneath the driver's seat, sputtered, then caught and spit gravel as it fishtailed onto Appleton Avenue, taking off in the direction opposite of the sounds of the approaching siren.

Al and I ran across the street and into a field. We were running hard. I stumbled and fell, easily breaking through a thin glaze of ice over a cold puddle. I was wet and cold; shivering as my fear crystallized in the freezing November night air. I caught up to Al and we kept running — blindly. There was a rustling sound, then a yelp. Al was down. A second later, I ran right into a twisted old section of rusty barbwire fencing; catching it at mid-thigh, I went down in a heap, pants and leg torn, right on top of Al.

"Get off me and cool it." Al responded to my squeal. "I think we can take it slower from here." He pulled down his leather jacket, smoothed his tight black pant legs and pushed back his hair.

We got up and kept going, jogging now, ignoring the pain from our encounter with the rusty fence and trying to pay attention to where we were headed. Fifteen or twenty minutes later we emerged from the field on Main Street and walked to my house.

An hour later, the other three pulled up in Grif's Chevy. They had been driving around town and not seen any roadblocks. We were safe for now.

We decided that enjoying our loot tonight was a bad idea. If we were caught drinking, we might be implicated in the crime of the century, okay the year, well the biggest liquor heist in Menomonee Falls (at least on this particular November evening). We hid the three bottles in a dresser in the workshop in my basement—the perfect hiding place. My dad had been gone for over a year, and nobody ever went into the shop anymore.

The next week of school began slowly. By Friday, we figured the heat was off, and we decided to enjoy our booty after the school dance. Who would get to join us? Russ suggested girls only and we quickly and unanimously agreed.

I walked to The Grill that Friday, looking good in my skintight white Levi's and new penny loafers, sans pennies (pennies would have been too strong a statement and I just didn't feel ready). We would go to the dance, charm a lady, pile into the Chevy, make a quick stop at my house for the booze (I had checked on it before I left), and go to Mike's mom's farm to party.

Later, during a slow song, "Only Love Can Break Your Heart" by Gene Pitney, I asked Cynthia to go out after the dance. She seemed anxious to go. Cynthia was hot, and though we both had been putting out feelers for a little while now, I still had that ever-present fear of rejection.

Mike and Russ also got dates; Al and Grif did not. The girls seemed okay with that, so off we went. When we got to my house, I quietly snuck into the basement.

I came out empty-handed. "It's gone."

"It's gone? What do you mean it's gone? I'll help you look," Russ said.

The three of us with dates were the most disappointed in this development, but rest assured, all five of us were shattered. We'd been looking forward to this all week, an eternity for a fifteen-year-old.

Russ and I went back into the basement but again came out empty-handed. The seven of them piled back into the Chevy, leaving me exiled in my driveway. This was punishment for my failure, and I understood that, but Cynthia went along with them. That just wasn't right. You'd think she'd only come along for the drinking! I'd hoped it was my skin-tight white Levi's that had attracted her attention. Maybe I should have gone with the pennies.

Later that night, I was awakened by the fumbling and stumbling of my seventeen-year-old brother, Jerry. It didn't take much of a leap to come to the conclusion that he and his friends had imbibed my stash. And it wasn't the first thing of mine he'd helped himself to.

"Are you drunk?" I demanded.

"What's it to you?"

"You're a prick! It's bad enough you used to steal my paper route money, but you stole my liquor."

"I didn't know it was yours. What are you gonna do about it? If you rat me out, you're in deeper shit. Where the hell did you get three bottles of booze anyway?"

"Asshole."

He rolled over, already snoring the snore of the cotton-mouthed.

I lay there feeling impotent.

Monday, I told the rest of the guys that my brother took the bottles from the basement. They shrugged it off, but it seemed a lot like The Big 4.

I didn't get thrown out of the group, but like a balloon with a pinhole, The Big 5 slowly deflated into something more like The Little 5. We remained friends through high school, but we were finding other interests, with girlfriends being chief among them. Cynthia and I began dating steadily. Maybe it was the tight white Levi's after all.

After graduation, all five of us kind of went our own way. Al had moved away before senior year. Russ went to work in a hardware store and married shortly after high school. The old horn-dog had apparently been house broken. Grif joined the Navy. The reunions became less frequent and the reasons for missing them more compelling, for all of us, I suspect. Even Mike and I, though we both went to college in Madison, didn't get together other than on the rare occasions we bumped into each other on campus.

For one night in November 1964, though, the group of five friends was a pack of thieves. We committed a crime, albeit a minor one. Thinking back, I roll my eyes at the sheer stupidity of it. Our complete inability to recognize that the consequences of getting caught far outweighed the reward of getting puking drunk was staggering.

But not only did we not get caught, it turned out we were never in any real danger of getting caught. I realized later that those sirens that night had nothing to do with us. Maybe one of the cows from the last farm within Menomonee Falls' city limits had wandered off and was wreaking havoc in the A & W parking lot.

On the other hand, we also never reaped our reward because what we stole was in turn stolen from us — irony or poetic justice, perhaps. Did I learn a lesson? Perhaps. But I never did have much of a proclivity for a life of crime anyway. That was the first and last time I stole anything. I suppose the reason is a fairly strong moral compass combined with an oversize fear of getting caught.

Along with an eye roll, I can't help but smile at the memory.

I've spent about thirty years of my adult life as a trader. One of the jokes I've often told on myself is that I could never seem to get my brains and my balls to work together. I often got ballsy with bad trades and timid with smart ones. Well, on that November night in 1964 I was very ballsy and very stupid. What's more, I was incredibly lucky. Had I been caught, my life might have turned out very differently. But I wasn't caught. So I can smile when I remember the leader of the pack, perhaps with the slightly different lyrics, "he took me to the liquor store ... that's where he left me, the leader of the pack." Vroom. Vroom.

1965

News that Shook the World:

LBJ Tells Michigan Grads to Build
Great Society

Martin Luther King, Jr. Leads
Alabama Freedom Walk

LBJ Sends 50,000 More Troops to Vietnam

Dylan "Goes Electric" at Newport
Folk Festival

The Beatles Play Shea Stadium
in Queens, N.Y.

Watts Ghetto Riots Leave 34 Dead

Malcolm X Assassinated in Manhattan

But More Importantly:

Tom Gets His Driver's License
Then Is Rocked and Rolled

No. 1 Song on July 23, 1965:

"(Can't Get No) Satisfaction"
by The Rolling Stones

No. 1 Song on September 4, 1965:

"Help"
by The Beatles

chapter six

HELP

"Take it in." Coach Pierce stood over me briefly before turning to leave the field.

I was on my hands and knees, gasping, light-headed, leg-achingly exhausted. I think I would have puked had I had the energy. I rolled over on my back and hungrily gulped the hot, humid air. How did Mother Nature know our practice schedule? Every year it seemed, the weather in this southeast Wisconsin town turned sultry on the first day of practice and didn't cool off again until well after school started. Help!

"Get up and run back to the locker room—helmet on!"

I struggled to my feet and ran—no, shuffled—across the practice field toward the high school across the street. As I came up on Coach Pierce, he stopped me, then grabbed my facemask and pulled me down to his eye level.

"Do we understand each other?"

"Yes, Coach."

"We won't do this again, 'cause next time you're gone, this year and next. Understand?"

"Yes, sir."

It was Friday, September 4, 1965, the last day of two-a-days. Classes would start next Tuesday, the day after Labor Day, and from then on practices would be right after school. But for the last two weeks, we'd been on the practice field from 7 to 10 a.m. and again from 5 to 7 p.m, Monday through Friday. Hitting drills, instruction, scrimmages, and sprints followed tortuous and tedious conditioning, day after day.

All of my practices went on for eight to ten minutes longer than my teammates'. When the last whistle blew and the team jogged off the practice field, I joined Coach Pierce on the goal line for 100-yard sprints. I ran until Coach Pierce had enough, or until I dropped — whichever came first.

The reason for my close personal bond with Coach Pierce was that we had a deal. We made the deal on Friday, August 20 after our mandatory team meeting. It was a fair and equitable deal, even a generous one given the fact that Coach Pierce, an assistant in charge of the offensive and defensive lines, could simply have gone to the head coach and had me kicked-off the team. But he chose not to; I'm not sure why. I always thought he didn't like me. He chose to handle it personally and privately. I'll always be grateful to him, though, unfortunately, I don't think I ever told him so.

Coach Pierce was five feet six inches and weighed about 250 pounds. He was a yeller, an intimidator, a big-bellied Buddha who loved the violence of the game, but also the purity of fair play. That latter realization came some time after. At the time though, with the myopic worldview of a sixteen-year-old looking through his navel, I just thought he was a sadistic prick. But he was more than fair in the way he dealt with my transgression, always answering the other coaches' questions by saying it was between him and me.

And what was that transgression? Drinking. On Friday night, July 23, I procured a cold case of Old Milwaukee from the liquor store through the back yard and across the alley from my house. How, you might wonder, does a sixteen-year-old high school junior-to-be buy beer? Well, this was Wisconsin, this was 1965, and hell, I looked at least thirteen, some thought fourteen. The simple answer is I would walk to the liquor store with my mom and carry home the case of beer she bought. One Friday night, she called the owner and asked if she could send me with the money for a case of beer. When he agreed, *Bingo*!

After waiting what I deemed an appropriate number of days, I grabbed the empties (in those days the bottles were returnable) and went back to the liquor store, saying my mom sent me. Whether the owner believed me or not is unimportant—he sold me the beer, but always in through the back door into the storage room. I never went to the front of the store. The trick was not to get too greedy and to replace the empties in the back porch before my mom realized they were gone.

So that Friday evening, I put a cold case of Old Milwaukee on the floor next to the kitchen table and sat down with my buddy Russ. Why Old Milwaukee? Well, because it was the beer my mom drank, because it cost only $2.59 a case. A couple of hours later, I put the empties on the floor in the back porch, belched, peed, and staggered off with Russ to the park. That evening, I was drinking with a purpose, not just because I was a teenager with an opportunity. After about four of five beers, I explained to Russ just why I wanted to get drunk. Before I knew it, the beer was gone, well after I'd reached my goal—I was gone too.

The reason? I'd just lost my job. I'd rolled a half-ton dump truck earlier that afternoon. I was embarrassed, humiliated, and of course, desperate to somehow keep it a secret. But that wasn't going to happen; one of the guys I worked with was a friend of my brother's, so he already knew; already had the ammo to taunt me, and the propensity to be ruthless. And Menomonee Falls was still a relatively small town; word got around.

How did all this happen? I was sixteen and though I'd had my driver's license for a couple of months, I had little opportunity to drive, as the family car was seldom available to me. However, in early July, I was hired to replace my older brother working at a topsoil business just outside of town for $2.75 an hour. So I started driving an old beat-up half-ton dump truck on the property, hauling dirt.

For three weeks I did my job, getting better every day. I was no longer grinding gears or stalling the truck. I backed it up hills of loose dirt right to the edge and dumped my load of soil without tipping the truck. I even took a trip off the property, delivering a load of topsoil to a lot in a budding subdivision of split-level clones. That was scary but fun, and I pulled it off without a hitch. I was getting confident, even cocky. Hell, I was sixteen and I was bullet proof. Or so I thought.

That Friday afternoon, I rolled a freaking dump trunk. It started when my brother's friend Scott pulled up alongside me on one of the tightly packed dirt roads and challenged me to a race. Why wouldn't I? I'd been driving this truck for three weeks; I owned it. Was I scared? Shitless! But I was more afraid of turning down the challenge, of showing fear, of being a punk. And of course this was neither the first nor the last of these kinds of choices, as proven by the liquor store incident described in the previous chapter.

My own, after-the-fact self-analysis is that courting disaster, and looking foolish as a result, was a conscious choice I made, like being the class clown. Choose the where and when they will be laughing at you, and you're still the one in control. This kind of self-analysis is much cheaper than going to a professional (and allows me to retain my amateur standing.) I'm kind of anal anyway, so what the heck.

So off we went. I floored the truck and powered through the gears, going after Scott. Of course it was idiotic to even attempt such a stunt, but given that I didn't want to back down, I should have either gone for it or settled for second place. Yes or no. Instead, picking maybe, I was tentative and hesitant, and coming out of a turn I went too wide, losing my right tires in the soft, deep shoulder. I panicked and jerked the wheel left, hard. The result was neither a skid nor a fishtail. The truck snapped left and tipped right. It rolled onto its right side then onto its top like a turtle on its shell.

I wasn't hurt, at least not so that I could see. Apparently I wasn't going fast enough to be thrown from that tough old truck that would have snickered at the idea of seatbelts. Actually, I hadn't even been going fast enough to roll the damn thing, except

I panicked, halfway through the turn. I saw the whole thing in slow motion, like a replay on the ten o'clock news; a knockout punch, mouthpiece flying, ending a heavyweight bout—and I couldn't look away, seeing myself take the hit.

Clutching the wheel, I tried to keep from falling into the passenger door as the mirror on it crumpled and cracked. As I was leaning right, a chain on the floor of the cab, its two-inch links coiled, rattling, its den disturbed, decided to strike. I have no idea how it missed me, merely hissing past my ear. Nor do I understand how it didn't break the windshield, slamming instead into the roof of the cab, coiling around the rear-view mirror so tightly that I was unable to wrench it loose. Perhaps I didn't try too hard. I've always been phobic about snakes, and the thought of that chain coming after me, was enough that I was perfectly happy to leave it alone, coiled around the mirror, in the warmth of a July sun.

Crawling out the driver's-side window, I checked to see if I was whole and wondered if I could get the truck back on its wheels before anyone noticed it was down, its tires spinning in a desperate attempt to let someone know that things were not as they should be, and it was my fault.

"Oh God, help me!" I pleaded.

After a while, Scott came around the bend. Even before he stopped his truck, I could see his eyes widen in shock.

"Holy shit! Holy shit!" Scott climbed down from his cab. "Are you all right?"

"Yeah, I think so."

"Your ear is bleeding."

"Really? I can't feel anything," I said, touching the spot, coming away with blood on my fingers. "I guess you better go get someone. I'll wait here with the truck. I am so screwed!"

"Holy shit!" It came out a rolling laugh as he climbed back into his truck and went in search of the foreman.

The next hour was spent getting the truck back on its wheels. The first fifteen minutes were spent cussing me out and asking me how the hell I'd managed to flip a goddamned dump truck. The truck's resurrection was accomplished with chains and a front-end loader. Amazingly, the truck wasn't badly damaged, the road being packed dirt. In addition to the broken passenger side mirror, the lip of the dump was gnarled and the roof was now a bit convex inside and concave out. Bottom line: it still worked, and very little money would be needed for repairs.

"You want me to drive the truck back to the barn?" I asked.

"No. Just go on home. We'll call you."

They didn't call, of course, and that's how I was fired. Later, I would receive my final check, minus the minimal cost of those repairs.

So I went home. As I recall, I walked; I tried to hitchhike, but with no success. The trip was about four miles, and I was in no hurry to explain why I was home early from work. It also gave me time to reflect on what had happened and what it meant. That's when I came to the conclusion that a case of Old Milwaukee would give me some satisfaction.

It didn't, of course. It made things worse, as it so often does. But on that Friday night, July 23, I bought that case of beer, put it on the floor next to the kitchen table, and with Russ' help, finished it off in a couple of hours. Then we walked to the park, across the street from the high school and up a hill from The Grill.

The park was where we hung out. We played softball and basketball, winners keeping the court. We hung by our cars; we met our friends. It was mostly a guys' hangout; mostly about sports, though we did want the girls in the stands when we had a game. When we arrived at the park that evening, there was a softball game in progress, so we sat in the stands for a while. In my inebriated state, I made my presence known. Kids giggled while grownups shushed. Looking back, I have to question my plan. How did I think public drunkenness would turn people's attention away from me and my embarrassment?

Eventually, the umpire called a timeout, turned away from the play, and directed his attention toward the stands. He seemed to move in an exaggerated, dramatic way as if playing to the back of the theater. Once more, I was witnessing the consequences of my own stupidity in slow motion. Removing his facemask, he grinned at me malevolently. It was Coach Pierce. Won't somebody please, please help me?

"I'm screwed," I said, loudly enough for the right fielder to hear. That was just in case Coach Pierce, looking into the sun, didn't know it was me. Meanwhile, Russ was laughing so hard that he was holding his sides, tears running down his face.

Pierce came around the fence, skirted the visitors' bench, and stood in front of me. "Mr. Alt, leave. Now."

There were a few measures of manhood that were critical in the small-town Midwest just before the "Revolution." To be seen as men, we needed to be able to handle a car (and by proxy, a truck), we had to be able to handle our liquor, we needed to be at least a passable athlete (even if not on a school team), and we had to show a basic level of comfort around the opposite sex.

To illustrate, the slightly pudgy, shy offensive tackle with bad skin, the one who was always seen carrying his books and a clarinet and who spent his Friday nights with his own fist, was not a man. The barely passing Grif, a pretty boy, with the baby blue convertible, who could drink and dance, was. In all likelihood, that studious, shy lineman was much more a man than our pretty boy or me or a lot of others who spent their time preening and partying and just passing through school. But that's not how we saw it.

The way I saw it was this: I'd had two strikes in one day. I'd rolled a truck—strike one. I'd gotten drunk—strike two. I was seen intoxicated in public by a coach, which could very likely lead to—strike three. I'm quite certain that in this situation, three strikes and you're out. And come to think of it, I hadn't had a date in a while. Damn, maybe I should just join the marching band, or German Club, or the Seminary. My God, I didn't really like Liberace, did I? I just couldn't seem to get no satisfaction.

After leaving the park, Russ and I headed to The Grill. We

feasted on Big Gs, burgers with George's special sauce (don't tell, but it was thousand island dressing), fries, and cherry Cokes. As I dipped my fries in ketchup, I worried about my future on the football team. Any chance that the few weeks till practice would be long enough for Coach Pierce to forget tonight?

No, there was no chance of that. The mandatory football meeting for all upper classmen was Friday night, August 20 at 6:30 p.m. Walking to the meeting felt like going to court for sentencing after I'd already been found guilty. As I shuffled into the classroom like a prisoner wearing leg shackles, all eyes were on me, and they had the look of a crowd at a hanging. Some were friendly, sympathetic, but most seemed twitchy, ready to vote thumbs down and excited at the prospect of seeing someone dangling.

Many of my teammates had shared a beer or two with me during the summer, but none had been caught. I guess the difference between a good kid and a bad kid is sometimes as simple as getting caught.

Fortunately, Coach Pierce kept my transgression between him and me. Looking back, I guess there is a pretty good chance that the other coaches knew about my little episode in the park but were willing to go along with Coach Pierce. At the time, however, I thought they didn't know. Maybe my coaches realized that taking away a healthy activity, like a school sport, was not the best way to prevent delinquent, destructive behavior. Naw ... that would've made them good guys. And that would mean I'd have to change my opinion, and I don't like to let facts get in the way of a good opinion.

The meeting, as it turned out, did not include my execution. Coach Pierce did, however, appoint himself my probation officer. Asking me to stay after the meeting for a few minutes, he categorized the incident as a mistake that must be paid for, but that, if not repeated, could be forgotten. Then he explained the details of my ensuing rehabilitation. He gave me a chance to get back on the good side. In short, he treated me like a man.

I met my probation officer after every practice. He was, it turns out, a good guy. In paying for my crime, I became as strong and as fit as I'd ever been. It was reflected in my season. I was fast on kick-off returns. I was a strong replacement for our senior running back, pounding on the tired defenders in the fourth quarter, even making some big hits from my defensive back position. I was no star, but Coach Pierce's punishment made me better than I would've been. His punishment was, in fact, preparation.

1965 was a pivotal year in my life. I turned sixteen, got a driver's license, started shaving, and began in earnest my journey toward manhood — a journey I hope to finish by my next birthday. Though my life was still insular, my vision still narrow, I began to notice things around me. We would become, this year, deeply entrenched in Vietnam. GIs barely older than me were wading through jungles while I ran wind sprints; they were dodging bullets while I dodged defenders. We began seeing those young men every evening in our living rooms. We were introduced to them by Walter Cronkite and David Brinkley, who forced us to see our reflections in their weary, jaded eyes.

I was beginning to see a bigger world, but was still, for the most part, self-absorbed. I continued to consider my place in my narrow universe to be of primary importance. I felt my missteps to be deadly serious embarrassments I couldn't imagine outgrowing. But gnawing at the edges of my consciousness was the knowledge that the next couple of years would determine whether I went to college or was sent to those far-away jungles.

I've learned that all those events in my little world, though mortifying then, were hardly significant in the larger story of my life, and were barely ripples in the greater world. Today, I look back at them and laugh at myself, a largely normal kid who made some silly decisions. I also look back in gratitude that I was fortunate enough to survive my own stupidity. I was one of the lucky kids who weren't pulled under by a few mistakes. Thanks for the help, Coach Pierce.

1966

News that Shook the World:

1st Acid Test Hosted by Ken Kesey

LSD Declared Illegal in US

James Meredith Shot in Mississippi

Bobby Seale and Huey P. Newton Establish
Black Panther Party

National Organization for Women (NOW)
Founded in Washington DC

Charles Whitman Kills 13 from Bell Tower
On University of Texas Campus

25,000 Anti-War Protestors March in NYC

US Bombs Hanoi for First Time

215,000 US Troops in Vietnam;
LBJ Says US is There to Stay

But More Importantly:

Tom Finds a Mentor:
A Five-Foot-Nothing Bespectacled
Tyrant

No. 1 Song on October 17, 1966:

"Reach Out — I'll Be There"
by The Four Tops

chapter seven

I'll Be There

I woke up, wiped the drool from my cheek, and got up from my desk. The bell had just ended my last class of the day, calculus/trig. It was Monday, October 17, 1966. I went to my locker in the senior-class hallway to drop off the books I didn't need and grab my jacket and English folder; I had a paper due tomorrow, which I had, of course, not yet started. This wasn't due to the senior blahs; those wouldn't come for a few more months. What I was doing was clinging ferociously to my exalted status as an all-star underachiever. I was an advocate of the attitude that one could not fail if one did not try. Adolescent? I couldn't disagree with you.

Every day, I power-napped in calculus. I just couldn't help it; try as I might, I couldn't stay awake. The teacher, a smallish, bald man who could have passed for human camouflage, may have been one of the most boring people ever born. He droned on, reading from the book in a monotone he could have marketed as an opiate. But he was a nice man, and on the previous Friday, feeling guilty of being disrespectful, I vowed not to put my head on my desk, no matter what. A few minutes later, I fell out of my desk onto the floor. Entertaining as it was for the rest of the class, I decided that laying my head on my arms was less disruptive, not to mention less dangerous.

Cynthia, my dark-eyed little hottie of a girlfriend, joined me at my locker. "Coming over tonight?"

"I have an English paper due tomorrow, so I don't know."

"You didn't start it yet, did you?" Cynthia was sexy and well built, with big black opals for eyes, but was also a very good, very serious student. I liked that she was smart as well as pretty. I was also perfectly content with being her way of rebelling against her strict, very conservative parents, especially her social climbing mother. Her dad, the guidance director at the high school, though not as superficial as his wife, barely tolerated my relationship with his daughter. (As a father, I can now see his point.) His remark, the first time I picked Cynthia up was, "I've gone through your school records, so I guess it's alright. Have her home by twelve." She later told me that he wasn't thrilled about my grades, but liked my IQ. But more than that, Cynthia was my first love and would become my first heartbreak.

"No, but I know what I'm going to write. At least I read the book." I looked left, but not right, and leaned in to give Cynthia a quick kiss.

From the right, from the men's locker room, I heard the voice of Mr. Pierce, who in addition to being my favorite line coach and Cynthia's history teacher occasionally shared the faculty lounge with Cynthia's father. "Alt, shouldn't you be at practice? And, Miss Schaller, don't you have somewhere else to be?"

After looking hungrily at the purple M on Cynthia's cheerleading sweater, I grabbed my stuff, closed my locker and headed to football practice. "I'll call you," I said over my shoulder.

Practice followed the typical routine: warm up, position drills, scrimmage and then sprints to finish. I practiced pretty well at first, broke a couple of runs, laid a safety on his ass (soliciting a couple of woofs from the offense), and once again asked to compete for the kicking job. I could kick our kicker farther than he could kick the ball, but he was a coaches' favorite. Truth be told, he was very accurate on extra points, but didn't have a very strong leg.

It may have also had something to do with a little stunt I pulled the first week of practice. While behind the special team practicing extra points, I hollered, "Jim Thorpe lives," and dropkicked a ball over their heads. Even though it split the upright and would have been good from thirty/thirty-five yards, the coaches didn't seem willing to focus on that part of the "incident." They focused instead on my insubordination and then on my ass while kicking it around the field. I was widely considered to be a clown, both in the classroom and on the playing field.

However, the practice began to go downhill when, during the scrimmage, Mike, the backup quarterback, replaced Bill, a fellow senior and our first team quarterback. Bill was not the most intrepid of warriors. If a player in a different color jersey so much as entered Bill's zip code, the ball went up for grabs.

Mike, a junior, was a bit tougher and maybe even a better athlete. But, in our offense, the quarterback primarily handed off to the running backs and threw the occasional pass. Bill had a better arm and Mike was inexperienced. What he lacked in experience, though, he made up for in cockiness, not necessarily a bad thing in a quarterback.

Anyway, the first play was a 12 trap, a counter to the two hole on the right side. It was the same play I'd busted for a couple of long runs. I was lined up at left halfback. After stepping left, I came back right and prepared to take the handoff. The ball hit me in the thigh pads—fumble.

From behind, our offensive back coach, Mr. Dees yelled, "Run it again. Alt, hang on to the ball."

We re-huddled. I glared at Mike, but said nothing. We lined up and ran the play again. Again, the handoff hit me in the thigh pads—fumble.

"Alt, get the hell out of there. Get me a back who can hang on to the ball."

I stood there for a second, waiting for Mike to take responsibility. He didn't—we'd talk about it later. I moved behind the offense. What I wanted to do was move to the defense and get a chance to put a hit on our back-up QB.

His face turned crimson and the scar on his upper lip came alive as Dees sneered; he seemed to delight in having an opportunity to dish out a bit of punishment on me. We didn't get along, and

I knew he thought I was a smart ass who belonged on the bench. He came up to me and pushed a football in my face. He wasn't a physically intimidating man, but he was about six feet two, so I had to look up just a bit to return his glare.

"Take this ball and run until I tell you to stop. If you drop the ball in practice, you won't carry it in a game."

"I haven't fumbled all year." I responded, a bit too forcefully.

I also reacted to the football in my face by clenching my fists and leaning toward him, wanting, for just a second, to take a run at him. Any good coach would've realized that it was the QB who was botching the handoffs. Still, Dees probably did know the truth. That was just the way he coached—if he liked you, great; if not, good luck. And, just in case I'd forgotten, the evil grin on his face reminded me that he did not like me, and he controlled my fate. I grabbed the ball and started to run. I thought that I should've decked the sadistic son-of-a-bitch. I wondered if Mike botched the handoffs on purpose. The runner behind me was his buddy. When I wasn't in trouble with the coaches, I played running back and safety. As in the classroom, I used humor as a defense mechanism to mask my insecurity and to cope with disappointment, but my coaches didn't share my brand of humor. I loved sports and wanted desperately to be better than I was. In a pick-up game, I could hold my own and sometimes even dominate. But when it counted I got nervous and my brain seemed to shut down.

I can see now that I choked; maybe not a full-fledged "cost us the game, in need of the Heimlich" choke, but a "not playing up to my ability" gag. I needed a coach to see my potential and give me a pat on the back, tell me he had confidence in me, instead of a daily kick in the ass. Obviously, my "I-don't-give-a-shit" attitude didn't exactly solicit that kind of mentoring. But I blamed it on the coaches. They were the grownups, after all.

On the other hand, I was a senior and deep down, I knew this thing was getting a little old. You might be thinking the same thing, having read this before. The chip on my shoulder was starting to get heavy. I still tried too hard and put too much pressure on myself in games while preparing too little in practice.

It mattered to me how I would be viewed as an athlete, but other things were creeping in as well. I'd started thinking about college. I'd always just assumed I would go but began wondering where and how. To that end, I had run for and been elected senior class president to help round out my resume. I began to look more broadly at the country and the world. Politics and war were becoming everyday issues, and large numbers of my generation were seeking and sometimes finding an alternate life. I wasn't ready to march or drop out yet, but I was always ready to challenge "the man." I did it the way I'd always done it; with a smart comment, a contemptuous grin, and an insolent shrug.

After practice, I showered and walked home. I grabbed some dinner, went to my room, and finally got to my English paper.

My paper, on Huckleberry Finn, was a commentary on Huck's relationship with the various adults in his life, his "role models" and what they taught him about the world. It fit quite nicely into my own mistrust of many of the role models I had encountered.

I've already mentioned my problems with authority, especially when that authority seemed both arrogant and arbitrary. I had many coaches who seemed to pick their starters based more on politics than ability. I met many adults who judged a teenager solely on looks. I had friends who were pretty good athletes but were completely ignored or buried on the bench by their coaches.

Anyway, I decided that writing about race in Huckleberry Finn would have been a bit too easy, and truthfully, I had little perspective on race and racism. Menomonee Falls was a very homogenous and insular little town. I think the first Black I saw was across the line of scrimmage. I enjoyed writing the paper and when I handed it in I remember thinking it was pretty good.

A week later, the graded paper was returned to me, an A-. It may seem funny that I remember this specific grade, but it's because of the teacher comments that came with it. It was a "very good paper, thoughtful, and showed original thinking …" And then this, "it could be better—you could be so much better—you can be whatever you want. I know you think you work best under the pressure of a deadline, but don't shortchange yourself. Work at your writing!"

The class was Senior Honors English. The teacher and author of those remarks was Miss Kemmeter. Miss K was five-feet-nothing and about 150 years old. She was a bespectacled, gray-haired tyrant. She only taught senior honors classes, so seniors were really the only ones who had much contact with her. Underclassmen shuddered at the prospect of taking her class, and her students dreaded the first day in her classroom as if about to face a firing squad.

She announced to her classes on the first day that it was time for them to grow up. They were no longer children, but would soon be college students. Therefore, they would be expected to read and write like college students. She demanded we read "actively," not passively, that we mark up our books, write notes in the margins, and dog-ear the pages. If, in class discussions, we regurgitated something from the book or echoed one of her comments, she chided us, reminding us not to tell her something she already knew. She was the best teacher I've ever had. She was the first adult to ever tell me "you can do this" and make me believe it. I could talk to Miss K because she listened, and looking back, I cherished my relationship with the woman.

Somehow that tiny gray-haired tyrant taught me about mutual respect and friendship between "unequals." I discovered the humor and compassion behind the curtain. She wasn't really so tough after all. She abided humor in her classroom as long as it wasn't disrespectful. Until I encountered her, I had not known there was a difference between the two. Miss K was experienced enough, competent enough, and confident enough that it wasn't about her, it was about us, and I trusted her. She would be there if I needed her.

I would love to say that Miss K merely found my switch and flipped it on. In truth it was more difficult than that. My mistrust, particularly in myself (after all, I'd been repeatedly told from a very young age by my parents, and teachers and coaches what a screw-up I was—what an underachiever I was—a real waste of oxygen!) made me stubbornly cling to what I was good at—screwing up and then making a joke of it. That was so much easier to believe than Miss K.'s message. So it took some time.

I wasn't instantly better on the football field or the basketball court or in my other classes. However, I began to work harder at writing, not waiting till the night before to begin my assignments. I got better. I received A- after A-. Finally, included in Miss K.'s critique was, "… these are A papers, but I want to see your best work." Another thing Miss K tried to teach me, I realize now, is the utter arrogance of doing less than your best, of thinking a half-hearted, half-assed effort is enough. Of course, she would have put it much more eloquently, but as forceful and helpful as her message was, I wasn't ready to hear it. I clung to the comfort of the commonplace, afraid to look over the edge. After all, what if my best wasn't very good?

Both as a seventeen-year-old and as a comic spokesman for the underachievers of the adolescent universe, I was compelled to challenge Miss K, the same way I did all my other teachers, coaches, and other adults who held sway. Interestingly enough, I think she understood this, but didn't give-up on me. She seemed to tell me to be the best me, unlike most of my teachers and coaches who said do what I tell you. And before I knew what happened, I had a mentor—me! The lack of adult role models up to that point in my life does not mean that I met no worthy or credible adults, but it did mean that I carried a certain mistrust and was unwilling to listen, to be taught. Miss K did manage to teach me though, hard as I might have resisted. I began to listen and to learn, and even to trust her. She didn't insist I act like I cared, but rather show her I cared, with good work. She tried to teach me not to be afraid of my talents.

Let me say that I wasn't a total screw-up. I was a pretty good student, with a B plus/A minus average. I earned an academic scholarship to the University of Wisconsin-Madison, primarily on the merits of my SATs (another testament to my status as an under-achiever). I was a decent, though not particularly accomplished athlete, and I was a leader of sorts, having been elected senior class president. I was, however, an under-achiever, flamingly mediocre, and I took a kind of perverse pride in that. You see—I could do pretty well without really trying.

I grinned (or rather, smirked) after acing a test I hadn't studied for. I would fly through an in-class assignment, then put my head down after looking around at confused, head-scratching classmates. Kind of an asshole? No question. But I was insecure, and trying to find some silly way of being as good as or even better than my peers. The reality, of course, was that I was afraid to really try—afraid that if I tried, I might fail.

Throughout my senior year, the bond between Miss K and me grew stronger. I found myself, only occasionally mind you, reaching out to her. She was always there. She was a stern taskmaster, demanding better and better work from me. You know what? I worked to give it to her; I strove to improve. I enjoyed her confidence in me and wanted to validate it. Even more, I reveled in the sense of accomplishment my work gave me.

Before Christmas break, Miss K gave us an assignment that would count as our first semester final. We could pick any of our papers from that semester, improve it and expand it. She warned us that it would be graded strictly—very strictly. I chose my early paper on Huck Finn and actually took it home with me and began working on it during break.

Amazing, the crazy old hag was right. One could actually get better by working hard, by going over the paper again and again. I aced that sucker, and I aced the course.

The second semester was even better. (I know I've leaked into 1967, but it's part of the story). Miss K's class was the highlight of my final high school spring. Okay, the academic highlight at least. There were some moments outside of school that were pretty memorable, especially for an old man with selective memory syndrome. I made small, incremental improvements in my craft.

Miss K was unquestionably the best teacher I've ever had. She treated her class of graduating seniors like adults, giving us a bit more rope and responsibility every day. For the most part, we didn't abuse that privilege. Rather we reveled in it, tired of the heavy-handedness of many of our teachers and coaches.

I was so ready to leave good old Menomonee High, so ready to leave "Monotony" Falls, but I knew there were a few people I'd miss. Most of them were admittedly of the female persuasion — one, as I mentioned, was about 150 years old. Recently, I've found my old senior yearbook and paged through it, reading some of the messages written there. My favorite was written by Miss K herself, "Hitch your wagon to a star, Tom, you are so capable."

As graduation loomed, I presided over an all-school awards assembly. In cap and gown, the seniors marched into the packed gym with me bringing up the rear, fumbling with my tassel. Miss K was by the door. She grabbed me by the sleeve of my blue graduation gown, signaling for me to bend down. While adjusting my tassel, she whispered in my ear, "If you need me, I'll be there. Now shape up." She then turned to a group of underclassmen with a gaze right out of Greek mythology. Two sophomores, if I recall, actually turned to stone. I, however, practically danced up the aisle toward the stage humming "look over your shoulder … I'll be there." During the assembly, a few students received small scholarships from local civic groups. I would introduce the spokesperson for each group, then listen as they extolled the virtues of their particular honoree. Twice, I was that honoree. I was totally surprised by the rewards, but not by learning that Miss K was the one who nominated me.

She said she'd be there for me and she was. There weren't many adults in my young life who were. Perhaps it was me pushing them away, all the while seeking their validation — little came. More than forty years later, Miss K is still there. When I feel cursed, or just like coasting, I read what she wrote in my senior yearbook. Then, I go pick out a star.

1967

News that Shook the World:

Israel Launches Six-Day War,
Takes Control of Sinai, Gaza Strip,
West Bank & Golan Heights

Race Riots in Milwaukee, Detroit
& Washington DC

"Summer of Love"
in Haight-Ashbury, San Francisco

Thurgood Marshall
Becomes 1st African-American
Supreme Court Justice

Che Guevara Killed in Bolivia

Packers Beat Kansas City 35-10 in
First Super Bowl

But More Importantly:

Tom's Senior Bash Ends in Crash ...
Mad Dash

No. 1 Song on June 1, 1967:

"Groovin'"
by The Young Rascals

chapter eight

GROOVIN'

Saturday June 1, 1967, was a beautiful day; the promise of summer rode on a warm gentle breeze. It carried first the smell of fresh mown grass, then the smells of working farms, then the happy chirp of crickets. Silos dotted the horizon in salute to the azure blue sky. We were headed north out of Menomonee Falls on State Highway 45 to a twenty-acre farm owned by Mike's mom. Russ was behind the wheel of his '65 GTO, burgundy with a black interior and a 389 cubic inch engine with three deuces and a four speed. The Doors' "Light My Fire" thundered from the 8-track. I cranked up the volume, drowning out the crickets, and sang along as the wheels kept time with the driving beat of the song. "Come on baby light my fire ..."

Grif and Al followed in Grif's '58 baby blue Chevy Bel Air convertible. Russ punched it, the three carbs kicked in and we were flying, getting air as we jumped a bump in the road. The Chevy coughed, then conceded, disappearing as we crested a hill. We were making our second run to the farm, getting ready for tonight.

The Big 5 was going to host a senior party tonight at the farm, nine days before we all graduated from Menomonee Falls High School. Yeah, we were still together and Grif was still driving that same convertible. But we decided that stealing the beer for tonight's blowout was just plain stupid (maybe we had learned a few things, though clearly, not a lot.) So, older siblings helped us procure a couple of quarter barrels of Bud, which were chilling in the farm's two acre, spring-fed pond. We'd collected $5 a head to cover the cost of food and drink. We'd grill burgers and dogs and there'd be chips galore, as well as a half dozen watermelons laced with just a splash of cheap vodka. Anything else was BYO.

The Big 5 included Russ, Al, Mike, Grif and me. Normally our parties were small and exclusive, but tonight the guest list had been greatly expanded. We were seniors, after all. Soon, there would be more on the horizon than softball games and summer jobs. Most of us would go to college at one of the state schools; a few would go "away" to school. Others would begin the drudgery of daily toil, and still others would join the service. A few ended up in that faraway war that was in our living rooms every night — Vietnam. Al went to Wisconsin State-Oshkosh, Russ went to work in a hardware store, and Grif joined the Navy but managed to stay away from 'Nam. Mike and I would be going to the University of Wisconsin-Madison.

All that was for later; tonight we'd party. The beer was chilling nicely and we were groovin' on this Saturday afternoon. We piled the eats in the barn and put the Vodka in the freezer and as many watermelons as would fit in the fridge in the upstairs apartment; the rest we piled in the sink.

Mrs. Usnick had built the barn just a year ago and the loft apartment was its coolest feature, and where we would sleep tonight — maybe not alone. Okay, not really happening, but a boy can dream. Mike asked his mom if he could have "a few" friends at the farm. She agreed if we kept it to a few and promised to stay put, car keys in pocket. Only The 5 would be staying in the loft for the night unless we had a special guest. Anyone else could sleep in the barn or outside. I'd hoped that Cynthia, my steady, would get permission to spend the night at a friend's. She was a junior, but had received special dispensation from The 5 and was allowed to attend. We wouldn't be getting it on in front of an audience, but the thought of her sleeping with me still held the appeal of the forbidden softened by a touch of sweetness.

All this involved, of course, a large degree of risk. Mrs.

Usnick had a strong propensity to visit the farm early on Sunday mornings — her church I suppose. Could we get up, clean up, and get the others out of here by 7:00 a.m.? Most likely not. Would we have this party anyway? Of course!

Looking back, I can only shake my head in wonder at the exuberant stupidity of the endeavor. But 1967 was a long time ago — a different world. We'd certainly begun to lose the innocence of the 1950s. It was a time of race riots, assassinations, Vietnam, and the drug fueled counter-culture of Timothy Leary, Jack Kerouac, and Alan Ginsberg, who advocated turning on and dropping out. Many young people were raging against the war, racism, against the entire American establishment. But in Menomonee Falls, Wisconsin, not so much. Even in small towns like the Falls though, high school seniors were coming face to face with a future that might include being drafted and sent to 'Nam. I suspect the draft is the major difference in the degree to which the youth of the sixties showed their disapproval of an inappropriate war and the youth of today. We had a very personal stake in it.

Browsing through the 1967 Periscope, the MFHS yearbook, one would find more "greasers" than hippies, more Elvis impersonators than mop-tops. It was a quiet, conservative community, clinging tenaciously to more innocent times and still controlled, for the most part, by the enemy — adults. Parents and teachers alike still used the rod so as not to spoil the child. But they were also, in ways that now seem incomprehensible, incredibly lax. Anyone pulled over for driving under the influence — minor and adult alike — was likely put back behind the wheel and told to go straight home. A minor would also have his alcohol confiscated. When we went out on a Saturday night, our parents asked few questions and the only warning might be that we were to be up the next morning ready for church. For many of us, the biggest risk in being caught drinking would be word of it getting back to our coaches.

But for this party, we entertained no such fears. High school sports were in our rear-view mirror, graduation on the immediate horizon. Other worries didn't really cross our minds. Even though we were in a somewhat rural area, the not-so-close neighbors would likely hear noise from an expectantly raucous party and report us, but we worried not. So while tens of thousands of young people were descending on "The Haight" in San Francisco, several dozen high school seniors were on their way to Usnick's farm in the Wisconsin countryside for the party of the year.

We didn't really entertain the possibility of calamities like arrest, damage to the farm, or worse, injury, even death, even though we would be combining fast cars, water, and fire with accelerants like raging hormones and lots of booze. As I've asked my kids more than once, "what were you thinking?" Clearly we weren't.

The party got started around seven, just before a beautiful sunset, the temperature a balmy seventy-two, the breeze a light fan. The spring-fed pond was cold, but a few intrepid swimmers made for the raft, one floating on his back with a beer in each hand. As I recall, no one was skinny-dipping, so alas, no nipple sightings.

Even though, as I mentioned, there seemed little to worry about, at least tonight, some kids, as kids are apt to do, started drinking pretty hard. I'm not sure what the motivation for "pounding" is, but I suspect a big part of it is to drink what you can before you get caught and have to pour it out. I mean I don't think most kids want to get drunk real fast, pass out, and miss the party. What's the fun in that? A few of the others drank fast because they didn't chip in and were scrounging from the rest of us. They drank fast before they were told hands off.

One such drinker was Chip, who didn't bring his own and would pay us later. Right! He and I had been kind of friends since third grade but I never really liked him (he may have felt the same about me.) We'd lived in the same neighborhood, been in the same classes, on the same teams, and had mutual friends. So we spent a decent amount of time together. He was a liar, a cheat, a thief, and a bully. So like I said, I never much liked him — in fact, he was a dick. But Chip is the driving force of this story.

Some of us with more experience approached the evening with a bit more nonchalance. Being one such savvy veteran, and one of the hosts, I was taking it easy. And, as a member of the Big 5, I was expected to conduct myself with an appropriate measure of cool. Plus remember, I was staying, so I could drink all night and not face an inquiring parent who might want to know just what the hell I'd been doing. And, by the way, Cynthia was not there, having a "family thing," so I was solo. That didn't mean I was looking to "score," but rather that I was kind of an entertainment co-chair by proxy.

I was, and still am, a neat freak, a "Felix." So, in addition to playing host, I tried to make sure cups, plates, bottles and such were thrown in the trash and not scattered about the property. The other reasons I did this were: 1) if some sort of authority figure or even neighbor showed up, maybe if the place didn't look trashed, the alarm wouldn't so readily go off, and 2) it meant less to do in the morning when we'd be tired and hung over, or worse, awakened by Usnick's mom.

Anyway, most everybody was enjoying the party. There was a lot of reminiscing as well as talk of the future. In probably one of the great, not to mention saddest ironies of the evening, some of us talked about and toasted three of our fellow seniors who weren't with us that night. They had each died in an alcohol-related traffic accident, two together the previous summer, and one just three weeks earlier. The back roads of Wisconsin could be perilous places in the sixties, especially those roads connecting counties with "teen bars" that served beer to eighteen year olds with counties that had only adult bars. Menomonee Falls was in Waukesha County, which had only adult bars, but Washington County, to the north, had a handful of teen bars. The back roads connecting those two counties were notorious, sometimes deadly.

Though not every senior was there, most of us were enjoying our bond, our commonality as high school grads, and eschewing the usual cliques. The gathering was nicely democratic. Personally, I liked that aspect. The truth is, that even though a few myopic teenagers may have viewed me as one of the cool kids, I never really felt like I fit in. Was I a jock, a brain, a nerd, a rebel, or cool? Really, I was a bit of all of them, and therefore none of them. But I never would have told anyone that's how I felt. Rather, I treated each clique with just a modicum of measured disdain, letting them know that I felt no great need to be one of them. The one main exception to this convivial community was, of course, couples in love, some of whom clung jealously to each other, and engaged in those sickening "public displays of affection." One such jealous lover was my old buddy Chip. The fly in the watermelon, however, was that the object of his affection no longer shared those feelings.

Kitty and Chip had gone out, but had recently broken up and she wanted nothing to do with him. The break-up apparently was not as mutual as Chip would've had us believe. This surprised no one, as Kitty was clearly out of his league, and most of us couldn't grasp the reason they were together in the first place. He wouldn't leave her alone and was fast becoming the pooper at the party. I suggested to Chip that he either leave Kitty alone or leave the party. He challenged me to a fight, but didn't really mean it, so, you know … nothing.

Chip would harass, threaten, and beg. Then he'd go off and brood into another beer, come back and start all over again. Finally at around 10:30 p.m., Kitty apparently said something to Chip that knocked him off that merry-go-round. He stomped away, threatening suicide, got into his car, and tore off, spitting venom and gravel. Kitty was crying into my chest, not for her loss, but for her embarrassment. Being eighteen, I admit to wishing, just for a moment, that our positions were reversed. You see, Kitty had big, and I assume beautiful … Never mind, Kitty was my friend and she needed me. She'd been my campaign manager when I decided to run for senior class president. I ran at the suggestion of my guidance counselor (more on him later) who thought it would fill out my resume for a college scholarship I desperately needed. Most of the rest of us were glad Chip was gone, thought he was maybe okay to drive and even snickered at the whole silly suicide threat.

Thirty or so seconds later, we heard the squeal of tires and the crunch of metal. Someone had hit something and it was close by. As a handful of us started running toward the sound, a horn wailed. About 200 yards ahead, Chip's '63 Impala was wearing a tree as a hood ornament. He was slumped over the wheel, but didn't appear hurt. You know how when you look in at a supposedly sleeping child, you can tell they're faking. That was my immediate feeling when we got to Chip's car; the angles and body language were wrong. We pulled him back and knew he was play-acting. Like I said before—what a dick! We were able to get his minimally damaged Chevy away from the tree (a young sapling that more than likely bore the brunt of the collision) and back on the road. He drove off, once again spitting venom and gravel.

Now I don't want to dismiss a possible suicide attempt so derisively. In my humble opinion though, Chip no more tried to kill himself than this is the Great American Novel. Anyway, did I mention he was a dick? And the whole drinking and driving thing was just as wrong, just as dangerous then as now, even if the legal ramifications were less perilous. But like I said, Chip's behavior that night drove this story and what happened after he hit the tree is what, in my opinion makes the tale worth telling.

We ran back to the farm and began organizing our escape. People piled into cars and left while a few of us pushed the kegs back into the pond, put out the fire, and gathered up the rest of the evidence and stowed it in the barn, padlocking the doors. We figured if no one were around, the police wouldn't search too hard when they got there. And they'd get there—soon; we could hear the sirens. Although the area was largely undeveloped, there were neighbors and the crash, as well as Scott's horn, had obviously been heard. At least that's what I think we figured;

we were pretty much in panic mode. So much for grooving'. We couldn't get away too soon.

There were now about twelve kids left and three cars; Mike's truck, Russ' '65 GTO and my '63 Corvair, and by mine, I mean the family car. We headed toward our wheels. Oops, make that twenty people; there were eight stuffed into my Corvair, seven girls and Ron. (Nice guy, and looking back, I think he may have been the first gay man I knew. He was in the back seat with four eighteen-year-old girls in various stages of inebriation, Kitty among them, pretty hot and pretty drunk, not to mention pretty vulnerable, and was acting … well, like one of the girls. And his hair was just too damn well quaffed all the time, even then.) Back to having eight people in my car … why? For God's sake, why? The white Corvair Monza was a small car, with red vinyl bucket seats in front, and room for maybe three people in back if they were small, maybe members of the Lollipop Guild. I have no clue why they chose or how they managed to stuff themselves into my little car, but it was too late to do anything about it. We had to leave.

I got into the driver's seat and pulled-out. Now the Corvair had "four-on-the-floor," and it had a very long throw from first to second gear and from third to fourth. Beth was in the middle of the front, left leg in the driver's seat and right in the passenger's, straddling the shift. Beth had come with Bill, a good friend of mine. But she didn't leave with him because his car filled quickly and, for the same reason I didn't empty the Corvair, Bill didn't make room for Beth. We needed to move fast. So I promised Bill that Beth would go with me.

The first time I shifted into second gear, I banged the inside of her left knee and she was required to accommodate the shift knob's slide into third base, I mean second gear. Beth was one of those "rah-rah" types, marching band, decorate the gym, student council types, with just a hint of nerd, and as such, she either drank too much too fast or just couldn't hold her liquor . She was kind of cute and kind of nice, but in that cloying, over-sweet way, so if you spent too much time with her, your teeth hurt.

Right now, she was drunk, and didn't seem to mind giving up so many triples; and as we drove on, the gearshift knob, with my right hand firmly attached, slid into third again and again. I may have been over-shifting. I don't clearly recall, but soon the third base coach seemed to be waiving me home. Beth had one of those "I'll give you just thirty minutes to stop that" smiles on her drunken little face. Who knew I was so attractive to slightly nerdy, clarinet playing, very drunk goody-goodies? Another stop sign ahead, a bigger smile? I had apparently discovered the use of a four speed as foreplay.

Meanwhile, the group in the back seat was trying to get one of the girls from the middle to a window. She was getting sick.

"Outside." I yelled. "Outside the car."

She lurched toward the window and hurled. The problem was, she'd forgotten to roll down the window. That's right, there were rivulets of things from her great gastric depths running down the inside of the window and pooling in the bristles that protect the glass from the frame. Now the rest of us were getting sick. One of the girls sprayed some perfume. It didn't help. It was even more cloying than Beth, if that's possible. Kitty reached over and bravely rolled down the window, trapping much of the offending odor in the door. Ron opened the other back window. I pleaded for quiet, not wanting to draw attention to us.

Christ, I wanted this one-car wagon train to end, but my carpool passengers were spread all over the Menomonee Falls map. I'd dropped off three of the girls and was driving down Pilgrim Road, when Beth announced that she had to pee.

"Can you wait?"

"No, I have to go now."

I pulled off the road near a wooded field where now sits the local YMCA or maybe a funeral home. Perhaps both have been built in this once open space and they're right next to each other. That would make sense to me, because when I was little, we had to swim nude at the Y, which I found more disturbing than embarrassing. It was mortifying enough, however, that I could picture kids saying, "Kill me, kill me now." Then they could just carry their bodies next door to the funeral home, where at least they would be wearing a suit.

Beth looked at me and said, "Come with me."

I looked at Kitty and said, "Go with her."

"No, you," Beth answered.

"How about Ron?" He's a guy, I thought, but maybe he's been to a slumber party or two.

"You have to come with me."

Oh my God, I thought. "Okay," I said. Again, I was worried about attracting unwanted attention. And, once again, who was to know that I was so attractive to a drunken nerd? Not Bill, I hoped. Finally, I recall thinking that this was creepy, not sexy.

I got out of the car and Beth crawled over the driver's seat, stumbling into my arms. A few steps from the car, and the road, Beth was ready to squat. I thought it better that we went a little farther and found a nice tree for her to hide behind. We found a private spot for Beth to answer the call.

"Hold my hand so I don't fall."

This was a level of intimacy I'd not yet achieved with a woman and was quite probably not ready for. But, I held her hand. She peed.

"What do I …?"

"Use your panties and then leave them. They don't have your name in them, do they?"

"No," she said as she fumbled with her shorts and her panties and then her shorts again. She giggled as she grabbed my arm and we made our way back to the car, her stumbling drunkenly, me shuffling as one with a head trauma. It was all a bit, well… not sexy.

Well, I got her home. While walking her to the door, she confided that this was the first time she had ever been drunk.

"Really? No."

Finally, it was just Kitty and me. Everyone else was safely in his or her home, and no parent had chased me down the street. We sat in Kitty's drive for a time, talking. I reassured her that she need not feel guilty about Chip. There was no way he really tried to kill himself and she shouldn't surrender to his emotional blackmail. He'd be a lot easier to ignore after graduation and then in a couple of months she'd be going away to school. She kissed me on the cheek, said thanks, and went in the house. It was about one o'clock in the morning.

The consequences of the party began to manifest themselves when I pulled into my garage. I had to clean the car, so I got a bucket of water and some rags. I rolled up the back window, cleaned it and rolled it back down. I did this over and over but was never able to get it completely clean. The next morning, on the way to church, my little brother rolled the window up, despite my repeated requests to the contrary.

"Ooh, what's this?"

My mom and I talked when we got home. She was very upset about the car and my driving privileges were revoked indefinitely and I was grounded for a month. Come to think of it, I was seemingly always grounded, and my sentences seemed commensurate with major felonies and not teenage indiscretions. I spent more time grounded than airplanes during an air traffic controllers' strike.

The next day in school, the Monday of our final week as high school students, I was called out of my first period study hall to the guidance councilor's office. He was, by the way, Cynthia's father, who had, after vetting me thoroughly, reluctantly allowed me to date his daughter. It appeared he was having second thoughts. Thank God she hadn't been at the party with me.

The principal was there, along with the head football coach and the other four. It was an ambush. Someone must have talked. Only Mike and I had earned letters in sports, and we were made to turn them in. There wasn't much else they could do to punish us. I, however, as senior class president (it was one of the reasons Cynthia was allowed to date me) was to deliver a graduation speech the following Saturday. They threatened to take that as well, but in the end relented.

In the next couple of days, the ripple grew. Someone had supplied a parent or teacher at least a partial list of attendees. Parents were notified and more varsity letters confiscated. Interestingly enough, not every athlete in attendance was made to surrender his purple M. It was, for the most part, the usual suspects. Yet no one who was punished gave up anyone who wasn't. This was, as I remember it, before the age of "plea-bargaining." The first one caught or accused didn't automatically trade his friends for his freedom, nor was he given the choice; he was made to man-up and take his medicine. It wouldn't get us our letters back anyway, and you just didn't rat out your comrades.

Even more interesting, no band member was made to give up their tuba or surrender their epaulet. Nor was any member of the science club or German club made to relinquish his or her beaker or purple and white umlaut. We might have missed an opportunity to file a discrimination suit. Or perhaps this was an early salvo in the nerds' revenge.

The penultimate repercussion of that Saturday night was the fallout from the peeing and discarded panties part of the evening's entertainment. Beth, in two of my classes, mostly avoided my eyes. When she did look at me, however, it was a look I couldn't read. Was it ... please don't say anything? Was it an acknowledgement of a shared intimacy? Hell, maybe it was ... could Bill borrow your Corvair?

Maybe she just didn't remember what happened. I was six years removed from my first date, and I still couldn't read a woman's eyes, not to mention her mind. I still couldn't do subtlety. To this day, I'm one of those men who usually has no idea what I did to get into trouble. Bill hadn't sought me out, so he probably wasn't pissed. When I saw him, if he wanted to know what happened, he'd probably ask. I'd probably tell him—mostly—though I'd probably not mention that the whole does she or doesn't she question had been answered. Would he understand that I never asked the damn question in the first place?

Cynthia, on the other hand, sought me out, and not just to say good morning to her guy. She wanted to know exactly what happened and why. She'd heard the stories and I had some 'splaining to do. With her hand on her hip and her left eyebrow raised in that disapproving arch (inherent or learned?), her look said, "You don't even carry my books, but you're holding her panties?" Why was Beth in your car and not Bill's? Why did you have to be the one to go with Beth into the field? I was tempted to tell her to ask Beth, or you know I'd rather be holding your panties, but this felt like one of those "discretion being the better part of valor" moments. Eventually, she accepted the explanation that I was just trying to get everyone home safely and stay out of trouble.

Finally, the party, I've come to realize, was a kind of watershed event. It was a party of many firsts and lasts. It was both an end and a beginning. More than the graduation — because it was just the kids — it marked the end of high school and the first step into a bigger world, one rife with both risks and rewards. For many of us, that night of groovin' at Usnick's farm was our last shared social experience. Perhaps the fact that it came to such an abrupt end was fitting ...

For me, it was the beginning of the end of my time in Menomonee Falls; the end of a significant part of my life. Interestingly enough, the changes in music seemed to dovetail with the changes in my life. Movement music muscled its way into our culture. It spoke of peace and freedom and even revolution, just as I would experience the freedom of living on my own. And as the Rascals said ... I really "couldn't get away too soon." Next year, I would be groovin' in Madison, but to a very different beat.

1968

News that Shook the World:

Rowan and Martin's "Laugh-In" Debuts

North Korea Seizes USS Pueblo
Levies Accusation of Spying

Viet Cong Begins Tet Offensive

26 GIs Charged in My Lai Massacre—
Only Lt. William Calley Convicted

Three College Students Killed in
Orangeburg, S.C.

Martin Luther King Jr.
Assassinated in Memphis

Robert F. Kennedy Killed in LA
by Sirhan Sirhan

Black Panthers Shoot It Out With Oakland
Police — Results in Several Deaths

Protestors Riot in Chicago — Mayor Daley
Gives "Shoot to Kill" Order

But More Importantly:

Tom's a Lover Not a Fighter
Is Jumped Anyway by a Couple of Frogs

No. 1 Song on November 30, 1968:

"Hey Jude"
by The Beatles

chapter nine

HEY JUDE

What I most remember is the arm. It was bare, hanging out of the shotgun window of the black 1965 Chevy Impala. It was huge—I mean huge! The car carrying it, and the presumably huge person attached to it, were turning around and coming back toward us.

I first saw the arm when the Chevy made a beeline toward us on State Road 67, south of Highway 18 just north of Dousman, Wisconsin. The driver tried to get us to jump off the shoulder. I guess he thought it was funny. Maybe he just didn't like us being there. Though jumpy, I didn't jump and my reaction was to mutter "fucking asshole." My travel companion didn't move, other than to extend his right middle finger in the air as the car sped past. This might have been the reason they were now turning around to make a second pass.

"Damn, Cricket; they're coming back," I hissed.

"Screw them." He challenged me with a look that said, "I'm taking no shit."

I'm thinking about the arm. Like I said, it was huge. I couldn't tell if it was muscular, or just big. If the former, we're screwed. I wanted to suggest to Cricket that we could perhaps take just a little shit … just this once. I was a lover not a fighter.

Oh, let me explain why we were walking on State Road 67 on Sunday night, November 30, 1968. We were sophomores at the University of Wisconsin-Madison, and had spent Thanksgiving at my house in Menomonee Falls. Cricket and I had met as freshmen. We had been assigned the same dorm floor. We'd become friends and I have the dubious honor or being one of the persons responsible for the first drop of alcohol to pass his lips. When inebriated, he had one of the most entertaining and infectious laughs I've ever heard. It was a kind of high-pitched bray, the kind that attracted stray dogs and the occasional female donkey. We also shared a common history, coming from working class families, and having earned our way to Madison with scholarships.

Our ride back to Madison fell through somehow and we decided to hitchhike back to school. It wasn't much of a decision, really. We were nowhere near a bus stop and couldn't afford a ticket anyway. We needed to get back to school (don't laugh, we went to some of our classes) and hitching seemed the only option. We convinced my mom to take us as far as US 94, an interstate running from Milwaukee west to Madison. She reluctantly agreed — this was, after all, taking her from her Sunday shows and her Manhattan(s) — and dropped us at the Highway 164 exit ramp in Waukesha, which was situated between Menomonee Falls and the interstate, and about 68 miles from Elm Drive B, our campus residence.

We tried getting a ride on the entrance ramp, but when that didn't work, we ventured on to the shoulder of the interstate. The only car we attracted belonged to a state trooper who told us to get off the interstate where hitchhiking was illegal. We complied, but of course returned to our post as soon as the trooper left.

We were cold already and desperate for a ride. As I mentioned, we had not anticipated having to hitch, and so were not dressed for the weather. Cricket was wearing a sweatshirt and I was wearing a light windbreaker, neither of which did much to protect us from the near-freezing temperatures and damp November air. A little later, the same trooper again caught us on the interstate. This time, he threatened us with arrest and took us to Highway 18, an old state road that paralleled the interstate and would also take us to Madison. At least in his car, we were warm.

"You damn college kids aren't above the law. Just stay off the interstate," he warned, dropping us off and pointing us west.

Now we were three or four miles from 94, so we couldn't go back. We'd just have to try to get a ride on this old route that went through several small towns. It was dark and freezing cold, and it being Sunday night, traffic was nearly non-existent. So we walked.

Dogs barked as we passed farms, yellow-white lights coming from their kitchens, dining rooms, or living rooms. Some emitted the intermittent glow of a TV tuned in, perhaps, to The Wonderful World of Disney. We couldn't see the fallow fields in the dark, their crops having long ago been harvested. But we could smell the dark, damp, loamy soil, sleepy but not yet covered for the winter, its acidity a nip at our nostrils.

After two hours and about eight miles, we saw a sign welcoming us to Dousman, Wisconsin, "The Frog Jumping Capital of the World." Now, I'd never been to Dousman before, never since, but apparently, every summer they hold a frog jumping contest and the winner is world champion. I'm not sure if frogs come in from all over the world to participate. I don't know if the winning frog wears a little crown, or maybe a little championship belt. Maybe he just becomes frog legs, though that is not something you would have seen on Wisconsin menus in the sixties, unless perhaps they were deep-fried. Maybe he gets sent to a French restaurant, maybe to France.

Even though we missed the contest, we continued into downtown Dousman to get warm. Nothing was open except a couple of bars, which, as far as I could tell, made up a quarter to a third of all business establishments in the downtown area. We ventured into one and were immediately tagged as strangers — underage strangers. We explained that we weren't trying to get a drink, just some warm air. We weren't welcome. This was, as I said, 1968, and much had happened to drive a wedge between the radical youth and mainstream America. Martin Luther King Jr. and Bobby Kennedy had been killed, their promise snuffed out; pros and antis faced off over the issue of the Vietnam War; campuses were rioting, cities burning; the Democratic National Convention in Chicago in August had been a virtual war zone. Each side blamed the other for the violence. Neither side trusted the other. On a more local level, the University of Wisconsin, an island of radicalism in a sea of conservatism, though highly regarded academically, was not in favor among the mostly conservative elements of the state. They thought it a den of sin, and the students were by and large seen as radical, hippie, "pinko," drug-using "faggots." Here in this bar and on the streets of Dousman, we were definitely the other side.

As we left the tavern, a hay wagon, pulled by a tractor and carrying mostly girls, came toward us down Main Street. Waving to us, they invited us to join them on their hayride. We climbed aboard the wagon, enjoying the warmth of our hosts, but coveting the hot chocolate. We rode a while, chatted with farm girls who found charm in the simple fact that we weren't local, and relished a hot chocolate or two, and then jumped off at the intersection of 67 (Main Street) and 18. Waving goodbye we resumed our journey west. It was a few minutes later when I first saw the arm.

I'm not entirely sure why the locals decided to hassle us. They hadn't seen us on the hay wagon with the girls. We didn't present as college kids, and certainly not as hippies. There were no peace signs or American Flags on our flared jeans. We didn't have long hair. Cricket was in the Naval ROTC program at school and groomed accordingly. Finally, we both came from towns not so different from Dousman except they were just a little bigger, just a little less remote. Maybe not being from Dousman was all it took to mark us as the enemy. Dousman was a bit more conservative, a little more insular, seemingly a whole lot more "… love it or leave it" in its thinking.

Anyway, like I said, the '65 Chevy came at us from behind, swerving close. Cricket saluted as they roared past, which, for some reason, upset them and they came back around. We stood our ground and waited. I also mentioned that I was a lover and not a fighter. Truth be told, I hadn't had a lot of experience at either, but felt a little more comfortable with soft caresses than clenched fists. I started thinking about a girl in my English Lit. class. Then there was this sexy little thing, Kathy that I'd run into at dinner in the cafeteria. And there was Christine, but we were just friends. I needed to focus. While standing our ground, I was seeking a possible escape route and noticed that a fence surrounded the field a few feet to our right. Apparently ground-standing was our only real option. You couldn't have taken just a little shit—just this once—huh Cricket? Quite possibly I was going to need at least some modicum of success as a fighter if I wanted to continue to grow as a lover. Shit!

As the car lurched toward us, a beer bottle shattered on the road, just short of us to the right. I think it was a Pabst. Figures. At UW, we drank Budweiser. The Impala screeched to a stop and the big arm disappeared inside the window, to open the door. Out lumbered a very big man. Seriously, what really happened, was out oozed a very, very fat kid, twenty years old or so. Meanwhile a tall, thin, pimply-faced greaser shot out of the driver's door, holding a beer. I was right—Pabst. He was Stan to his friend Ollie; Ichabod to a guy that practically needed a crane to get out of the car. The good news was: this guy was really fat; even better: there appeared to be only two of them; however, the bad news was: I might have to fight one of them. Cricket, in stark contrast to his wingman—me—was a fighter. Not only was he in the Naval ROTC program at Madison, he was also on the wrestling team. We nicknamed him Cricket because he had a big, muscular torso and long skinny legs.

"Hey dude, don't let me down," Cricket said in his best half-time voice.

"Which one of you shit heads gave me the bird?"

"That would be me, fat fuck," Cricket responded. I mentally rolled my eyes. Perhaps he might rethink his ambition to pursue a career in politics or the Diplomatic Corps after his stint as a naval officer.

I noticed Cricket slowly, subtly shortening the distance between him and his new friend (moving in for a handshake — possibly of the "Bro" variety?) and instinctively followed his lead. I had Cricket's back just as Stanley had Oliver's. Shit, where did he go? Oh there he is. I wonder if he realizes that when behind Ollie, he kind of disappears. Maybe like me, he's a lover and not a fighter. Not likely with that lunarscape of a face. I tried smiling at him anyway. His reaction was to change the grip on his beer bottle; apparently he'd just become more interested in swinging it than swigging from it. Clearly, we had little in common and pursuing this relationship would be a waste of time.

The two wrestlers, one a Sumo, began circling, sizing each other up. Actually Ollie was pretty much rooted in place and Cricket moved around him in an ever-tightening orbit.

"I'm going to break your ... ooph!" Ollie never finished the threat. Cricket had landed a perfectly placed kick to the fat man's crotch. I think his whole damn foot disappeared for a split second. Thank God it didn't get it stuck in there. That could have quickly turned the fight in our opponents' favor.

"You mother- ... oh!" A second well-timed bulls-eye to Ollie's future fatherhood made him swallow another threat.

"Pardon me?" Cricket was taunting, dancing. Ollie was sucking air, clearly in pain. Even as a potential victim, it was hard for me to watch. My face scrunched up in a grimace as my knees involuntarily came together and my hand went down in a protective caress. I reacted the way every man reacts every time he sees another man take a hard shot to the balls. It's visceral. We feel it, all the way up into our throat.

Ollie, with both hands cupping his boys, took one more hard shot to the groin. He went to his knees making a kind of gurgling sound — or was that me? I swallowed my guys back down where they belonged and turned my attention back to Stan. As I did, I noticed that he'd had taken a defensive position behind his open car door. He too was hypnotized by the action in front of us, his attention fully on his fallen comrade. I moved in and gave a hard kick to the door, slamming it against him. Stan yelped and dropped his Pabst. He raised a hand in a "no mas" gesture (or perhaps he needed to go to the bathroom.) Meanwhile, back to the real fight ...

Cricket had Ollie, who was on his knees, by the hair, threatening to kick him in the face. "Why'd you have to fuck with us? What did we do?" Cricket gave him a hard push, and the fight was over. Ollie lay on the pavement, part road kill, part oil slick.

"Leave us the fuck alone, or I'll really hurt you!" Cricket yelled over his shoulder as we resumed our journey west. Cricket is my hero 'cause he's so brave and strong. He was the trail boss or wagon master on this two-man wagon train going west. Only we didn't have a wagon. We could really have used a wagon. We still had about sixty miles to go.

Looking back, I realize that Cricket did the right thing. He did what was necessary to get the fight over quickly and save our asses. This wasn't about fighting fair; it was about getting the hell out of there in one piece. Back then, though we continuously looked over our shoulders for our new friends, or worse, friends of our new friends, we couldn't look back. We still had a long trip in front of us. Once again, the cold stabbed at us through our thin clothing. It stung more because of our sweat—Cricket's from exertion, and mine mostly from fear. We were chilled to the bone.

Again we walked, past farms with restless livestock and barking dogs. We didn't see a car in either direction for an hour. We talked about knocking on a door and asking for a place to stay. We discussed slipping into a barn to spend the night. We even hatched a plot to rustle a couple of horses and ride them to Madison. We wondered if we might be hung if caught. Finally, a car approached from behind; we hitched and hoped. It slowed, considered stopping, then sped away, not willing to risk picking up two strangers on this cold night. So on we walked, tired but too cold to stop.

Sometime past midnight, and just over seven hours till my

first class, we walked into downtown Jefferson, Wisconsin. Jefferson, built as a transportation hub at the confluence of the Rock and Crawfish Rivers, called itself the "Gemütlichkeit City." The German word means comfy, cozy, homelike. Jefferson even had a World War II prison camp on its fairgrounds for German POWs. We could only hope to find even a bit of that quality in a little city fast asleep.

In an inauspicious introduction to the city, a freezing drizzle began just as we entered the downtown area. We wedged ourselves into a corner phone booth and farted for warmth. That's how frigging cold we were.

Looking around, we saw a George Webb's sign. Actually, it read "G org Web." This 24-hour greasy spoon served ulcerating coffee, greasy burgers, eggs, chicken soup with an armada of clotted grease floating on its surface, and chili from a can. It was a Midwest chain with locations in Milwaukee and Madison and even one in Menomonee Falls that I'd visited, specializing in après drinking cuisine. We went in and ordered. I had bacon and eggs; Cricket went with the chili. While gratefully clutching my hot coffee, I made a note not to get back in a phone booth with him—no matter how cold I was. I'd seen the chili's effects before. We nursed our coffee, spending as much time on our stools as we could. It being a Sunday night, there were only a couple of drunks, I mean patrons in the place, and the counter man didn't seem to mind us hanging around. He did give us the occasional, over-the-glasses, you're not from around here look, and seemed to time a passing patrol car. Maybe he was worried that we might start an anti-war protest or maybe pull out and burn an American Flag and there weren't enough able bodies in the diner to beat the shit out of us if we did.

We were discussing the improbability of getting a ride at 2:30 on a Monday morning, and had all but decided to stay in Jefferson (at George Webb's?) until it was light, when one of the patrons drunkenly offered to take us to Cambridge, another little town about twelve miles down the road to Madison. We

quickly calculated the odds of a head-on collision at near zero
(there were no other cars on the road!) and figured any accident
would likely be a one-car, and we'd more than likely just end
up in a field (remember we were university students, we could
do these calculations in our head.) We followed the drunk out
to his pickup. I lost the flip and had to ride middle (and no, this
was nothing like the trip home from Usnick's farm—he never
even got to second base). Being two sheets to the wind already,
our chauffeur rode with the windows down and his head out the
window. I swear his tongue was out in a kind of canine smile and
his ears flapped in the breeze. It did smell better in the truck, but
we were once again freezing.

Cambridge is a cute little Wisconsin lake town. Koshkonong
Creek runs through the town on the banks of, believe it or not,
Lake Ripley. By the time we thanked our driver, it was about 3:15,
and nothing was stirring in this little town. We tried the doors to
the Catholic Church, but found them locked. We may have been
better served by staying in Jefferson. With no other option, we
started walking. We were zombie-like, shuffling quietly through
a world of silence. No animals stirred and no dogs barked. After
what seemed an eternity, and just as the skies turned from black
to midnight blue, the birds began to wake. They fluttered about,
their chirps announcing the coming of a new day, chasing us
from behind.

At the intersection of Highway 12/18 and old State Road 73
was a service station and donut shop. We lingered awhile, and
then set up shop at the intersection. After a half hour or so, a
woman not much older than us stopped and offered us a ride.
She was commuting to her job in Madison. I don't remember
exactly what she looked like, but she was beautiful, an angel,
and her name was Judy. She didn't hate or mistrust us because
we were college students; in fact she envied us. We told her she
could be as easily as us, if she wanted to. I don't remember where
she worked, but she told us she was early enough that she had
the time to take us all the way to our dorm.

We drove into Madison on the Beltline highway. Just off to our right was the capital building, backlit by a sun just breeching the still, dark waters of Lake Monona, one of four lakes that make the Wisconsin capital an isthmus. (The others are Lake Mendota, Lake Wingra and Lake Waubesa.) We turned on Park Street, eventually passing below Bascom Hill, the center of the university, and turned onto Lake Shore Drive.

The school is built along the northern shore of Lake Mendota, the biggest of the four lakes. The campus was still sleeping on this November morning and, except for the occasional lonely jogger, was deserted. The campus of the University of Wisconsin is widely regarded as one of the nation's most beautiful, and I fully appreciated its beauty this day.

Judy dropped us off right at the front door of Elm Drive B. She lingered just a moment, ogling the three-story, blonde brick building as if it were a resort in a glossy magazine ad. The time was 6:50 and I had plenty of time to make my 7:45 class.

"Hey, Jude, thanks."

1968 was a tumultuous year in America. It often seemed that the very fabric of our country was being torn asunder by the anger and mistrust of the generations, by Vietnam, by the radicalization of students and colleges, by the hippie movement, by drugs. During the fall of 1967, violence erupted on the Madison campus when student demonstrations against Dow Chemical recruiting on campus turned into skirmishes with the University and Madison police. Active participants were beaten and dragged from campus by very enthusiastic Madison police in full riot gear.

Even those of us who were merely watching this morality play were hit smack in the face by the tear gas used as liberally as the policemen's night sticks. That was just the opening salvo in a battle between students and the authorities for the soul of the university. Violence raged on campus for three or four years.

Mostly, I observed; questioning the efficacy of such actions, and also feeling that many of the student activists were spoiled kids biting the hand that fed them. In the spring of 1968, however, I was on Bascom Hill between classes when the tear gas canisters were again popping and a skirmish had broken out right there on the hill during an anti-war march. When I spotted an undercover policeman beating and kicking a helpless coed, I reacted by tackling him, then grabbing the girl and running into the chaos.

For many young people, college students in particular, the world seemed on the verge of imploding. For this reason, many chose to merely "drop out." Every day, I passed a construction site on campus. The wooden barrier surrounding it was covered in posters, fliers, slogans, and protest art. One that has always stuck with me was: "Due to lack of interest, tomorrow has been canceled." I liked both the biting humor and the sad resignation of it. I remember seeing the same thing in the faces of many of my fellow students.

My experiences that Thanksgiving weekend hitchhiking to Madison with Cricket both reinforced those feelings and brought them into question. We were attacked for being different—for being the other guys. We also found a common bond in our approach to and our aspirations for our lives. I did realize I was lucky to be in Madison and not Dousman, let alone 'Nam. I felt grateful for the opportunity to be a part of a great university during an incredibly interesting time. I felt a renewed energy and drive to use my time well and broaden my experiences. Mostly I realized I couldn't fuck-up my student deferment.

Having thanked our angel, Judy, who had not let us down, we climbed the stairs to McNeel House and I unlocked the door to my room as Cricket continued down the hall. I grabbed my towel and headed to the shower. The hard, hot water warmed and renewed me. I got some more towels and covered the drains, then sat down in the warm water and fell asleep. Soon, I was awakened by other students with early classes. I went back to my room and crawled into bed. The hell with it, classes would still be there tomorrow.

1969

News that Shook the World:

Nixon Sworn In as 37th President

45 Injured, 184 Arrested in SDS-led
Takeover of Harvard's Administration
Building

Neil Armstrong's "Giant Leap
for Mankind"

Manson Family Goes on Murder Spree

Ted Kennedy Leaves Car & Mary Jo
Kopechne in Water at Chappaquiddick

Woodstock: Peace, Love, and Music

1st Draft Lottery Since WWII

But More Importantly:

Tom's Whole "Lover" Thing Hits
A Snag or Three

No. 1 Song on August 31, 1969:

"Honky Tonk Woman"
by The Rolling Stones

chapter ten

HONKY TONK WOMAN

Joe held the door and I brought in the last two cases of Bud. It was Sunday, August 31, 1969. Tomorrow was Labor Day and on Tuesday morning, fall classes would begin at the University of Wisconsin. It was the perfect reason for a party. Though maybe we weren't the perfect people to host it, we thought: what the hell, why not.

My roommates and I were starting our junior year in Madison. We rented a typically furnished (it even had the requisite, almost iconic ratty couch on the front porch), five-bedroom student house off campus for $300 a month, and by converting a basement room into a sixth bedroom were able to get our rent down to $50 a month per person. The squabbles over whose beer it was, how much peanut butter someone ate, or why did you use my milk to eat your Cheerios hadn't started yet, and we were feeling young and free and friendly. Hell, we were in Madison, Wisconsin and not the Mekong Delta.

Our only worries, or so we thought, were who to invite and that our landlady not find out about the party. The former was obvious: not just anyone would be allowed to drink the beer we paid so dearly for, the Bud $3.99 a case. The latter had more to do with the previous tenants' last party than our first. Apparently, someone at the party decided to redecorate, and when we arrived the day after to begin moving in, we found the kitchen stove had been moved via the window into the back yard, the flexible gas pipe dangling from the sill. For some reason, this upset Mrs.

Szoshkavitch, and she became a bit party averse.

But we partied nonetheless, right on the heels of Woodstock, which happened August 15–17 in Bethel, New York. A few of our guests had been to the festival of peace, love, and music on Max Yasgur's farm. One didn't remember much, and two returned without their companions who had yet to make it back. So with "Long Time Gone" by CSN playing in the background, the first hugs and handshakes were exchanged and the first beers popped. By the time The Rolling Stones' "Honky Tonk Woman," the number one song in America at the time, was blasting, the party was rocking.

The party presented, for me at least, one other minor predicament. I invited Christine, a very good friend, for whom I had recently been having feelings of a rather un-platonic nature. I know this, because a couple of my female buddies, still good friends forty years later, never caused my pulse to quicken or my mouth to dry. And I sure as hell never caught myself fantasizing about how they looked naked. I'd had to acknowledge these feelings two days earlier when Christine called to tell me she was back in Madison and asked me to pick her up at the sorority house where she'd be living. I couldn't believe how excited I was to hear her voice, and how palpable my longing to see her again. During lunch at Ella's, an iconic Madison deli on State Street half-way between the campus and the Capital, she told me she broke it off the night before with her boyfriend, a defensive end for the Badgers, and he was none too happy. I was.

Meanwhile, Steve, one of my roommates, bumped into Kathy, a girl I had been seeing for about six months, and with whom I had just broken up, and invited her without asking me. He wasn't aware, of course, that I'd asked Christine, and was unconcerned with whether Kathy's presence might be uncomfortable for me. At the party, I noticed Steve paying a lot of attention to Kathy, and in my opinion, he'd had a thing for her while she and I were dating, but honored the "guy code" and did nothing while we were together.

Now, though, I was sure he was hitting on her. This was okay with me. In fact it was a good thing, keeping her away from me and allowing me to concentrate on my naked images of Christine.

But not as good as I thought. Kathy had apparently spent the time telling Steve how I used her and then cast her aside when I was done. He decided to defend her honor and address the injustice I had perpetrated upon her. This is when things got a tad uncomfortable, even a bit embarrassing. After several drinks, and only a step or two from stumbling drunk, Steve decided to confront me publicly about my really shitty treatment of Kathy. Excess alcohol caused Steve, like a lot of people, to lose his hearing, as well as his short-term memory, forcing him to make his points quite loudly, again and again ... and again. Our year as roommates was starting out just dandy. The party was actually the fulcrum separating two stories, one about Kathy and me, and why we really broke up, the other about Christine and me and how we got together.

As I said, Kathy and I dated for about six months, after meeting in the lunch line in the commons that served meals to both our dorms. I wasn't very good at "chatting up" a girl, but well yeah, I chatted her up. Honestly, we didn't really date so much as we slept together.

Our relationship started in February during the Black Student Protest on campus. Demanding the right to establish a "black" curriculum, the 164 black students were joined by eight to ten thousand white students in demonstrating against the University. The protest succeeded in shutting down the school for several days until the regents called in the National Guard for the first time in UW history.

During this downtime, Kathy and I spent a lot of time indoors protesting existing conventions against premarital sex and clothing and the like, while outside, about twenty percent of UW students were protesting the existing tenets of education as prescribed by the university. When we wandered back to classes, the university, under siege, and with the National Guard on duty, looked like an armed camp. The statue of a seated Abraham Lincoln at the top of Bascom Hill and in front of Bascom Hall flanked by army jeeps with 50-caliber machine guns pointing at us was more than a bit surreal.

I looked like a prune, in need of rest and hydration. I absolved myself of wrongdoing in this arrangement, because from the very beginning, I told Kathy that I was seeing others and that we weren't in any way exclusive. I rationalized that this made me a straight shooter and allowed me to enjoy our purely physical relationship without guilt. I wasn't, I thought, using Kathy. We were using each other to our mutual benefit. We were, in the words of Bob Seger, "workin' on our night moves." (Yes, I know this song is not the title of this chapter, and didn't come out until 1976, and its inclusion may be seen as a tacit acceptance of a song not born in the sixties.)

Sure, there were tears and questions, as well as suggestions that we actually "go out" on Saturday night for a change. She told me often that she was tired of being my Sunday to Thursday girl. The fact that I balked at these suggestions didn't seem to be a deterrent to our continued liaisons and allowed me to believe that we were together for the same reason. My self-absorption kept me from realizing that her feelings for me were perhaps stronger and that our frequent unions may have been for her more about love than sex. She was giving me this great gift because of her feelings for me, and in the hope, I suppose, it would stir similar feelings in me. For my part, I guess I treated Kathy kind of like my honky tonk woman and paid attention only to the stirrings just south of my equator.

God, you have no idea the difference in the intensity and frequency of those stirrings in a twenty year old and a sixty year old.

Sorry, I digress. Anyway, Kathy and I spent a lot of time together doing some thorough and exhaustive research into the various condoms available on the market. There were some uncomfortable moments to be sure. I met her at The Pub, a bar on State Street or The Nitty Gritty, an Eastside establishment that was a favorite of the hippies who lived in the student ghetto known as "Miffland." Sometimes I would bump into Kathy between classes while walking down Bascom Hill with another girl.

There was the time she came up and kissed me on the mouth, marking her territory, while I was having lunch with a girl from my English class on the patio of the student union, overlooking Lake Mendota. Then, looking over her shoulder, her incredibly short dress barely covering her cute behind and fluttering even higher from a gust off the lake, she waved and said, "See you tonight." These meetings were somewhat rare occurrences, because I didn't spend a lot of time around the class buildings, not making it to many classes that semester. I spent much more time studying Kathy's anatomy than anything else.

It was the spring of '69. The students at the University of Wisconsin, the vanguard of the movement, were protesting the war in Vietnam. We had tried to run Dow Chemical, the manufacturer of napalm, off campus the year before. We trampled convention, the comfort zone of the military industrial complex, a more dangerous enemy to some than the Vietcong or Red Chinese. Revolution was in the air, wafting on the notes of movement music and the sweet smell of reefer. We were listening to songs by The Doors, Steppenwolf, and The Rascals. We were singing along to "Revolution" by The Beatles and "Get Together" by The Youngbloods (not your older brother's rock and roll). Hermann Hesse's "Siddhartha" and Ken Kesey's "One Flew Over The Cuckoo's Nest" were the favorite reads. Kesey's novel about an asylum in the Northwest was and still is one of my favorite books, and reading it under a tree on Bascom Hill was how I studied for my math final that semester. With a beer in my hand, the sun on my back, indifference in my heart, the endless, green, tree-lined campus spreading before me and the languid blue waters of Lake Mendota lapping my toes like a favorite dog, I had little time for class most days.

Anyway, I had to rest during the day, because I would probably be sneaking into Kathy's dorm room again that night, booting her roommate down the hall. I wonder why she never liked me. Remember now, this was the old days, when getting caught in a girl's dorm after hours could get both parties kicked out of the dorm. And as freshmen were required to live in a dorm, they would effectively be kicked out of school. Kathy was a freshman.

When the semester ended in early June, Kathy went back home to Green Bay. I stayed in Madison to work and for summer school. I was paying for a wasted spring semester, at least academically. It seemed a good idea to regain my academic standing and retain my draft deferment. Honestly, I thought I'd miss her. She was bright, funny, cute, blonde, about five feet five inches tall, with long thin legs and heavy breasts, and amazingly enough, available to me.

But she didn't give me a chance to learn if I'd really miss her. The very first weekend, she visited. That was the weekend I reached my sexual peak, June 13–15, 1969. Looking back, with no small amount of sadness, I'm quite sure of it. Somehow, Kathy was free to visit every weekend. So she visited the next weekend and the weekend after that, even though I said I had other plans. On that weekend, we fought and we... well you know. Finally, the first weekend in July, I told her not to come, as I wouldn't be in Madison. When she couldn't convince me otherwise, she went all Dow Chemical on me and dropped a napalm bomb of her own.

"I'm late and I've never been late before. I might be pregnant. I have to come and talk to you." This was Wednesday night.

"How can you be pregnant?" I asked, stunned. "We always used a condom, and you have a diaphragm."

"I don't know, but I'm scared. Please!"

"Okay. See you Friday," was all I was able to get out.

Now who's scared? I'm a college junior-to-be, Kathy, nineteen, would be a sophomore. I couldn't sleep, had no appetite, and went forty-eight hours without an erection, which has to be some sort of record for a twenty-year-old. I was a zombie, shuffling through my workday, and at night alternately staring at the TV, my beer, and the ceiling .

I couldn't really grasp the future this might bring to bear, but knew I couldn't abandon Kathy now; it's not how I was made. Together, we at least had to get from what might be to knowing for sure. From there, if she was pregnant — and yeah, I wondered if it was mine — we'd have to decide what to do about it. I'd stick it out to whatever end. It was my duty. I had to. Why? I guess because that is what I thought a heroic kind of man would do; the kind of man I needed to think I was, never leaving a damsel in distress, especially if it was my distress. Flashing back to 1963 when my dad left, and the lesson he taught me by abandoning us, I knew I wouldn't leave. If I did, I wouldn't be that hero, but would instead be my dad. Or maybe it was my Catholic upbringing ... the whole reap what you sow thing. At any rate, this was now much more than just "... going upstairs for a ride."

Kathy arrived in Madison at about 5:30 Friday afternoon after making the 135-mile drive from Green Bay. I was sitting on the front stoop, still dirty from work. Kathy jumped out of her red '66 Skylark, grabbed a bag from the back seat and bounced up the steps. She was wearing cut-off jeans so short they were teasing me with the hint of a tan line and a gauzy peasant blouse. My head moved involuntarily to the rhythm of her bounce. Noticing this she smiled wickedly and her left nipple winked at me — I swear it. She gave me a quick peck, crinkling her nose at my ripeness. I was amazed that she could be such a little seductress given the sword over our heads.

"How are you?" I asked, two very different emotions at play.

"Okay. No change."

"C'mon in. Grab a beer. I'll grab a shower."

The physical chemistry was there, though charged by a different electricity. I jumped into the shower. A couple minutes later, Kathy handed me a beer as she joined me. I held her and watched the water pool between her breasts. The forty-eight hours were up. We wandered, naked, down the hall to my room. There was no chance of us being seen. Though I had five roommates, four were home for the summer, and the fifth was working.

The sex, I must admit, seemed more like lovemaking. It was more tender, more emotional, but darkened by a tint of dread, a touch of desperation. I felt a different kind of urgency. It was still great. Maybe we were just getting better at it, learning together. I understood more clearly that I was happier when I pleased her. I don't know if she was a virgin before we met, didn't really care to know. Neither of us were sexual rookies, we'd both had some experience up to, if not including, intercourse, nor were we grizzled veterans and there was the occasional fumble. Over time, we had become more sure of ourselves, each other and enjoyed the discoveries we each made about the other. Everything else seemed as always, except the post-coital conversation.

"How could you be pregnant? I don't understand. We're careful to the point of paranoia."

"I don't know, but I haven't been with anyone else." She'd obviously heard an unasked question in my voice. "If I'm pregnant, it's yours."

"Have you seen a doctor?"

"No, I'm afraid to go to our family doctor. He would tell my parents."

"Let's go to the student clinic."

She didn't want to go, and this gnawed at the edges of my mind. I remembered thinking that the clinic of a major university in 1969 wouldn't be shocked by a coed asking for a pregnancy test, and they would respect her privacy. This would at least be a way to find out for sure. I also knew they occasionally performed abortions as a form of civil disobedience.

Early the next morning, Mrs. Szoshkavitch awakened us when she walked into my room to take down the curtains for washing.

"Hello, Mr."

"What the ...?" Kathy covered us both with the sheet. There is something incredibly sexy about the way a naked lover clutches the sheets so modestly to her breast. I appreciated her covering me as well. Did I mention I was twenty? Well, I was still greeting most every morning with the little soldier at attention, saluting the rising sun, and on this particular morning, the landlady.

"Mrs. Szoshkavitch, you can't just walk into my room."

"I'll be just a minute. I'll re-hang them this afternoon." Sophie Szoshkavitch, a recent Russian immigrant, was having a hard time grasping the concept of tenant privacy. She grabbed the curtains and left the room. Could Mrs. Szoshkavitch see our reflection in the window? Looking back, she seemed to linger a bit longer than necessary, and left the room with the curtains in her arms and a hint of a smile pulling at the corners of her mouth.

Awake now but not ready to get out of bed, Kathy and I test-drove another condom.

"We have cereal but no milk." I called over my shoulder. "You want a couple of eggs?"

"Why don't we go out for breakfast?"

"I'm broke." I said turning to face Kathy who was entering the kitchen. "I get paid Tuesday." Why is it that the first time a woman spends a night at a man's, she takes one of his shirts? And why is it so damned sexy? The above questions are rhetorical. You should know why, but if you don't it really doesn't matter. You just need to decide if you like her better in one of your T-shirts or a white dress shirt. I like the dress shirt because it has a buttoned or unbuttoned option. Kathy had picked an old basketball jersey and that was good too, especially from the side.

"I'll buy," she said, sliding into my arms. That morning in my kitchen in Madison, Wisconsin, lust was in the air, and the appropriate body parts pointed up; the laws of gravity held no jurisdiction over us.

Afterward, we drove to Country Kitchen on Park Avenue and The Beltline. I was wondering why Kathy only wanted to talk about her possible pregnancy on the phone, and still questioning her unwillingness to go to the clinic for a test. Truthfully I was aware how easily she manipulated me; naked, she owned me. When it was just her detached voice on the phone, she plied me with guilt and fear. I cared for her and wouldn't intentionally hurt her, but knew ours was a finite relationship; more passion than love, and like a candle, in burning it would consume itself. We slid into a booth and ordered. She played the fingers of my right hand like a piano. I wanted to pull away, but didn't.

"Kathy, I can't stand not knowing for sure. Why don't we go to the clinic? Next week, get here early and we'll go Friday afternoon. Or we could go to the hospital today."

"It's not an emergency."

"It's sure starting to feel like one."

"If I'm pregnant, I'll still come back to school in the fall."

"Look, I know this is mostly about you, your body, your choice. But it affects both our futures. I can't just walk away from this, but I'm not ready to be a father and you want to go to law school, right? If you wait too long, you limit your options."

"Oh God, Tom, I don't think I could have an abortion."

"Do you think you could have a baby? I mean now?"

As the summer dragged on, I wanted more and more to pull back, maybe pull away. When sensing this, Kathy talked about her possible pregnancy; then and only then, unless I brought it up. This went on for two months.

I was going out of my mind, wrestling with the implications of an unwanted pregnancy and desperately hoping it was all a dream. This was never part of the whole college experience I'd foreseen. When she was at home, she used it as an open invitation to visit; when she was with me, she knew exactly how to distract me.

Admittedly, I was easily distracted; after all I had the attention span of the twenty-year-old male. But, what had begun as a feeling became a suspicion and then an open question. Did she ever really think she was pregnant? I hadn't said it aloud yet, but it had been echoing in my head for a while.

Even now, though I hadn't thought about it for years, I'm

unsure of the answer. My belief has always been that she made the whole thing up. The week before Kathy was to return for her sophomore year, she called and told me she had her period. The relief I heard in her voice was drowned out by my own. As I was telling her how happy I was for her, I was silently whooping it up.

"My God, Tom. What a relief! Will you help me move into my apartment on Saturday?"

"Sure." I said. "What time will you get here?"

"Early. I'll call. See you."

After getting settled, Kathy asked me to spend the night. I knew if I did, that would be taking advantage, something I felt I hadn't yet done. The line then—and it sounds callous even as I write it—was I didn't walk away from my mistake. I stayed all summer when the possibility of an unwanted pregnancy loomed large. But now I had to go, and wouldn't string her along for one more taste of honey.

"Kathy, I can't. Listen I think we should stop seeing each other."

"Why? After what we've just been through ..."

"I'm sorry." I reached for her, but with arms crossed in front of her, she pulled away. "Bye Kathy." Neither of us even bothered to say let's be friends. I closed the door quietly and walked away. I had been hijacked and held hostage for two months by a fake pregnancy, so why did I feel like such an ass?

Looking back over time, I probably underestimated Kathy a little bit. I probably didn't appreciate how good she was to me, but have come to realize that our time together was for me as much about the intimacy as the sex. I'm not saying she was the one, but I cared for her more than I was willing to admit to her or me. I'd been hurt before, and this was a bit of a change. Yet I certainly didn't relish hurting her.

More likely than not, Kathy was just one chapter in my life. It was sweet, sexy, and scary all rolled up in one and made the summer of '69 one I'll not forget. Fortunately, UW is a big campus, and we didn't bump into each other often. I guess the bottom line was I liked Kathy, but really had a thing for Christine. Now that I knew Kathy wasn't pregnant and had ended it, I was free to explore those feelings. The following night's "Welcome back to Mad-town" party was a good time to start.

As I said, I didn't see Kathy often that year. However, I did see her the very next night — at our party. That was a little rough. Thanks, Steve.

Meanwhile, back at the party, I was sitting in an old armchair with Christine on the floor in front and to the side of me, forearms crossed on my thigh. This was a little after Steve confronted me, which incidentally Chris wasn't there to see. We were having a beer and talking. We'd always talked so easily, so honestly. Though I spent most nights last spring with Kathy, I spent a lot of time with Chris as well. If we bumped into each other in the cafeteria, and didn't have a class to go to, we'd sometimes stand and talk for hours after lunch.

She was smart and funny, tall, with brown hair and eyes, and beautiful full lips. She was very feminine, with a narrow back and tiny waist. She had small breasts and though I'd not yet seen them, I sensed they were perfect. We'd become really good friends. We could talk about anything, became each other's confidante. Neither Kathy nor Chris' boyfriend liked us spending so much time together, but it was innocent, and anyway, they needed to get over it.

While I was in Madison during the summer, Chris was back home in Chatham, New Jersey commuting to New York City where she worked in a law office. I was barely conscious that my feelings for Chris were evolving that summer into something more than platonic, and had no confidence whatsoever that she might share those feelings.

Okay so maybe we, and by we I mean me, weren't honest about everything. I never told her how I really felt. We talked occasionally during the summer and exchanged a few letters. In them, she complained about the lawyers in the office always hitting on her. It may have been a bit disingenuous. Sitting next to me now, she was bitching about her date last night, as well as the fact that a couple of her ex's teammates had already jumped into action and asked her out. I bitched a bit about Kathy, but mostly teased Chris. "Oh poor little Christine, so many men want you. Those damn lawyers. But you like dating football players. Maybe you can work your way up to the captain. You're just a little 'jock-sniffer' aren't you?"

"Oh, go to hell!"

"Maybe you can find a football playing lawyer." I think Chris liked my smart-ass irreverence and I made her laugh. I feigned a slight cockiness and often wore a little smirk that said I got the joke; mostly because deep down I worried that the joke was on me. Occasionally, my taunts found the soft underbelly and were not well received. This may have been one of those times. A "you know, it had sounded a lot funnier in my head" moment. Truth be told, these zingers had an edge to them, sharply honed by more than a little jealousy. The thing is, Chris and I could say just about anything to each other, exactly what we thought or felt. So she'd get over it.

"We gonna win a fucking football game this year?" someone asked.

"A couple," I said. The Badgers had gone 0–10 and 0–9–1 the last two years. They really sucked; the Saturday treks to Camp Randall becoming for many students more about a party than about the game. "But ask Chris, she knows the football team really well."

"How about you and your little Lolita?" Chris decided to fight back. "You sure you can live without her?" She always had a bemused expression on her face when she brought up Kathy.

"I can see anyone I want, and the sex was great."

"That's it? That's enough?"

"Yup. Another beer?" She nodded, and I went into the kitchen for a couple of Buds. When I got back, Kathy and Chris were deep in conversation, each giving me a knowing little smile, one after the other. Women, no matter their age, or yours, apparently have the innate ability to look at you like a teacher handing back a bad test. I remember thinking: this can't be good, so I wandered through the house and into the backyard, clinking bottles and chatting with some of my fellow Badgers. I bumped into Steve again.

"What the hell Steve? You don't know what went on between Kathy and me, so why don't you just mind your own fucking business."

"She told me."

"She told you what? And why do you assume she's telling you the truth and I'm not? We're friends for Christ's sake. You want to talk about this, come talk to me when you're sober." A little sensitive? Maybe I was. But I hadn't told anyone about the pregnancy scare, not even Christine.

The Friday after the party, after our first week of fall classes, two of which we shared, Chris and I were parked on a leafy street just outside the entrance to the zoo. It was a warm night, the crickets in good voice, the breeze sweet with a hint of summer's end. The windows of my 1960 Buick LeSabre were open, though truth be told, the right rear one was always open. For $50, I didn't demand that all four windows actually rolled up. I'd worry about the window in due time, probably after the first snow. Maybe I'd even get around to taking the old plates off and registering the car in my name … maybe not. Maybe I'd get the breaks fixed… maybe not.

Our conversation settled into the usual complaints about men and boys. Finally, I lost patience with the same old same old. "Dammit, Chris, I'm so tired of listening to you complaining about your guy problems. I don't care. I want to be your problem."

We sat in heavy silence, her no more stunned than me at the words that had just erupted from somewhere inside. What seemed like a long time later, she leaned into me and kissed me. Good God this is what had been missing! I was home. That first kiss was like a baby's first taste of ice cream. I was hooked.

I shivered with the smell and feel and taste of her. Our mouths seemed designed one for the other.

"What took you so long?" She asked.

"I didn't think you … what a waste of time."

Just like that, we were a couple.

Just like that we found ourselves becoming more intimate, more physical. I told Chris that because our mouths fit so perfectly together it meant nature had designed us so that all our parts would fit perfectly together as well. Though this was one part kidding and two parts line, it seemed true; we fit — perfectly. I didn't ask Christine if she was a virgin but she told me she was, and I chose to believe her. It would have made no difference. I knew she wasn't promiscuous. Honestly, I felt special to be her first. The first time we made love, I asked her: "Are you alright?"

"Yes," she said. "Yes!"

I was referring to birth control. She thought I was referring to her being a virgin and whether she felt any discomfort. Okay, I've given away the ending, but come on! We were two reasonably bright young adults yet our communication skills, not to mention our common sense, left a lot to be desired… don't ya think? The story is still worth telling, if only for the sad irony of it all. Just a few weeks earlier I was sweating out the possibility of a pregnancy, despite the fact that we never walked in the rain without a raincoat and an umbrella. Now I was running naked in the rain. And all I could think of to say was, "Are you alright?" In communication, clarity is key. Come on!

Amazingly, when Chris began feeling sick a couple of weeks later, neither of us thought, "Oh, God, no, not a pregnancy!" Perhaps she did know or at least fear pregnancy, but didn't let on. After going to the clinic, and a few days later, being admitted to the university hospital, Chris was visited by a sweet elderly doctor who gently asked her if she could be pregnant. The answer was of course yes. The test, like many others in college was true/false. The result … true; we aced the test. I wondered momentarily if I could use it to boost my GPA.

Now, of course, we needed to decide what to do. I was no more ready to be a father than I had been six weeks ago, even though obviously I was much more mature — remember the kind of decision-making that got us to room 228 of The University of Wisconsin Hospital in the first place. However, I was more willing. I was in love with this woman, not just in lust. But believing that Chris had the most at stake, I deferred to her. The doctor advised her that there was a way to end the pregnancy without calling it an abortion, which was illegal at the time, and he was willing to do that for her. He would submit a diagnosis that would exclude pregnancy, but call for a D&C for other medical reasons I don't remember well enough to articulate.

While most students were gone for Thanksgiving break, Chris had a medical procedure to end her pregnancy in its eighth week. Had she gone to term, we would have become parents in June of 1970, and I would have a forty-year-old son (for some reason, on the rare occasions when I think of it, I always think son). According to the hospital records though, Chris had not been pregnant, did not have an abortion, and her parents' insurance was never billed for her hospital stay or for the birth control prescription she left the hospital with. Residual guilt or not, it was absolutely the right decision.

This was no small event in a young life, but we seemed to shrug it off easily. Our relationship did not wane, but burned bright hot. For the rest of the semester, the rest of the year, the rest of 1969 and into 1970, we spent day and night together laughing, loving, and learning about each other. Chris, by the way, picked a white T-shirt of mine, and I remember her nipples dotting each 'i' in the word idiot. And yes, they were perfect.

I'm absolutely certain I could have identified her while blindfolded, using only my finger tips, or even better, only my lips. We made plans and promises. She even met my family. This was a big step, an even bigger risk. I worried my family would scare her away. It's not like we were trailer park trash, though. We didn't even own a trailer. Seeing where I'd come from didn't make her run. Perhaps she figured that I had enough going on and with her help there was no way I'd go back there. She even confided to my mom that she wanted to marry me.

Chris' pregnancy and abortion were quickly followed by another seminal event in our lives. On December 1, 1969, we listened to the first draft lottery at a campus bar along with a hundred or so other students. I won! I was thirty-three in the lottery and as soon as my student deferment expired would be called to military duty, and, I was certain, to Vietnam. We commiserated with the others with low numbers, congratulated those who may have escaped, then went home and made love, tenderly and not without tears.

By the way, remember that broken wrist I mentioned in my first story? Well, because I hadn't had it fixed, but opted to play with it broken, it would require surgery, which of course I wouldn't have done until after my eligibility passed. So, an apparently stupid decision by a fifteen-year-old turned out great. During the spring of my senior year at Madison, I was required to report for my draft physical in Milwaukee. They were wasting no time. If eligible, I would be called immediately upon graduation. But, because of that broken wrist, I failed the physical and was therefore ineligible for induction into military service

When the school year ended in June, Chris again went back to New Jersey. I drove her to Chicago. We went to see the musical Hair at the Schubert and spent the night at a hotel. We made love, tenderly, and then she lay in my arms and cried at the thought of leaving. I, of course, did not cry, though I may have gotten something in my eye.

The next morning, I drove her to O'Hare for her flight home. I again spent the summer in Madison. Unlike the previous summer, no one visited me every weekend, and I missed her ... terribly. We did talk often and she wrote almost every day. In one letter, she mentioned that her mom would make her wedding dress — amazingly this pleased me; did not terrify me — and as always, she loved me.

I made it through the summer and anxiously awaited her return. I'd rented an apartment I thought we'd share. We'd spend our senior year together as a prelude to the rest of our lives. The minute I saw her, I felt the difference and found it hard to breathe. She ended it with the old "it's not you it's me." For the second year in a row, she ended a relationship on the first day of the fall semester. I wondered if that's what she told her boyfriend the previous September, and thought ironically that he and I now had something else in common. Then I tried to recall if I'd used that line when I broke up with Kathy. I didn't. Even today I find little truth in it.

The campus didn't seem as big that school year, and I bumped into Chris often. Each time hurt. And when I'd see her talking to another guy, the wound, still open, stung more, salted with jealousy. She even visited me a few times, late at night, at the gas station where I worked. On many of those occasions, after I'd turned off the lights and the pumps and locked the doors, the visit turned physical. We still seemed to fit perfectly together, at least in my mind. Each of these times hurt more, and built up scar tissue on the backside of my soul. For me those nights were more about love than sex. This time the stirrings were centered north of my equator, not in my pants. I allowed her visits to continue, allowed her to use me, because I wasn't strong enough to stop them, and I was hoping to re-ignite those same stirrings in Chris.

I did not. Her visits became less frequent, then stopped, and our college years ended without so much as a goodbye.

Just like that, it was over.

I realize that my story about 1969 has bled into the 1970s, but I think I needed to finish it, at least to the degree that I can. I am aware that, at least for me, there has been no resolution, no answer to the question why. The need for an answer became less urgent long ago, no longer tinged with bitterness and hurt. It is now just a casual wondering why, wondering what happened.

It isn't the loss that I mourn, for I have gained much more, but rather the reason for it all that I crave. I've wondered if perhaps, she viewed our relationship as I saw mine with Kathy; wondered if she was just using me. Maybe she just used me for the sex and that makes me a stud. Okay, probably not, but I'm trying to get something out of this. Perhaps she was more in love with the idea of being in love than with me. Maybe it's just part of a life built of ironic symmetries. Maybe it's karma. Maybe I was just her honkytonk guy.

Today, on the forty-first anniversary of Woodstock, images of that time dance on the languid blue, early morning waters of Lake Michigan, which, just like Lake Mendota did so many years ago, lap at my toes like a favorite dog, as the sun warms my face. My iPod is loaded with 1960s music, my heart flooded with memories. It has certainly been a long and winding road from there to here. I am who I've known, what I've been, what I've done, and what's been done to me. It happened long ago as I came to be a man through the ten years that ended in 1969. It was a pivotal decade for me and for America. We lost our innocence, our virginity … our youth.

EPiLOGUE

If you've gotten this far, then you know that the stories were about growing up in the sixties. Though I hadn't thought of it in this way before, while writing this book, I've come to believe that there are really two different sixties. First of all, there is the actual decade of from 1960 through 1969. And then there's the sixties! They're a bit different and are a moving target, but are largely defined by Vietnam, the anti-war movement, campus unrest, drugs, hippies, communes, and the ever-evolving musical beat to which we marched. This culminated perhaps at Woodstock in August of 1969. The sixties were also marked by more assassinations, racial strife, and burning cities than any other decade.

At any rate, although the two sixties certainly overlap, they are not necessarily aligned. The first couple of years of this seminal decade were really an extension of the 1950s. They were still drive-in restaurants and drive-in movies. They were still innocence and Elvis. I think they may have ended on November 22, 1963, when President Kennedy's assassination hijacked that innocence.

A few weeks later, right on the heels of that tragedy, the Beatles invaded and conquered America. I remember going home for Christmas break my freshman year of high school being barely aware of the Fab Four. Shortly after returning to school in January 1964, the Beatles had three of the top four records on the charts. Change had come.

There was no turning back. The status quo, as well as the establishment, was being challenged from all sides it seemed. Millions marched; music went "movement." Our minstrels not only went from singing about puppy love to free love, but urged us to change, even revolt. Did the music mirror the movement or ignite it? I'm not sure, but they certainly marched in lock step.

I moved through this decade from childhood to manhood. I listened to, sang to, and danced to its music. As with most of us, it spoke to me, even spoke for me. As I said in my introduction, listening to this music evokes vivid memories of the past. It can change the rhythms of one's heart, cause it to beat in time to the songs of our youth.

If you, too, are a child of the sixties and you listen to the number one song of August 3, 1965, I'm betting you will not only remember what you were doing, but relive it. As the sounds of that song echo in your ears and its rhythms become your heartbeat, you will once again see, feel, and taste the past, if only for a moment.

I will argue to the end that the best music ever made was made in the 1960s. But if you were a child of the 1970s, or the 1950s, you would likely disagree. So if it's the 1950s you're all about, go find your reading glasses (after you've turned the house upside down looking for them, check to see if they are hanging from that beaded chain around your neck) and a well-lit room, find a song on your MP3 player from August 3, 1959, turn it way up so you can hear it, and relive a memory.

I'm listening to one of my favorite songs from 1965, "Just a Little" by the Beau Brummels. "So I'll cry just a little 'cause I love you so. And I'll die just a little 'cause I have to go … away." We've all had to leave that time behind, some, like me, reluctantly. But with music, we can always go back, if just for a little while. We were all children and though unique, all share similar experiences: a first date, a first kiss, a touchdown or a goal. We all made some monumental mistakes—many of them the same ones. I made a bunch and at the time, I doubted anyone had ever been as stupid or as embarrassed. I not only survived the stupidity of my youth, I've found joy in the memory of it and can actually look back and laugh.

The decade and the music may be different, but two things are very likely the same. We messed up and we survived. So I would suggest you do two things today: listen to a song you loved as a teenager, and enjoy— maybe even laugh at—the memories it evokes. Revel in the music and the memories. Smile at the success of surviving yourself.

Acknowledgements

Publishing a book, as I've learned, is no small task.
I couldn't have accomplished it without the assistance
of the people at Windy City Publishers.
Thank you for all the invaluable help.

I also want to thank a few others ...

First of all, Miss Kemmeter, my high school
senior honors English teacher, was the first person to
believe in me and make me believe in myself.
Thanks, Miss K.

My sister, Mary, gave me endless love and encouragement.
Thanks, Sis.

My children Erin and Sean are the stars in my universe,
and I want very much for them to be proud of the old man.

Finally, my wife, my love, Jeanne, who has stood alongside me
through thick and thin, is the reason I finished this.
Thank you for your patience and your love,
and for only occasionally giving me "that look."

giving2green

The giving2green symbol indicates that the user has committed to giving monies to the many organizations dedicated to the fight against global warming, decreasing greenhouse gas emissions, saving our rainforests and wetlands, and fighting water and air pollution.

giving2green gives 100 percent of its proceeds to supporting the organizations fighting these battles. Because we feel that saving our planet and the people, plants, and animals inhabiting it is one of the most critical challenges we face today, we request that all our authors commit their support as well.

We feel good about making a difference. Every little bit helps, and today's businesses should step up to the challenge of not only doing their part, but setting an example—not just because it's good for our environment, but because it's the right thing to do.